amazing crochet lace

NEW FASHIONS INSPIRED
BY OLD-FASHIONED LACE

|doris chan|

Copyright © 2006 by Doris Chan
Photography copyright © 2006 by Potter Craft

Published in the United States by Potter Craft, an imprint of
the Crown Publishing Group, a division of Random House,
Inc., New York.
www.crownpublishing.com
www.pottercraft.com

POTTER CRAFT and CLARKSON N. POTTER are trademarks,
and POTTER and colophon are registered trademarks of
Random House, Inc.

Library of Congress Cataloging-in-Publication Data is
available

Chan, Doris.
    Amazing Crochet Lace: new fashions inspired by
    old-fashioned lace/Doris Chan.—1st ed.
        p.   cm.
ISBN-13: 978-0-307-33975-1
ISBN-10: 0-307-33975-0
1. Crocheting—Patterns.   2. Lace and lace making—Patterns.
I. Title.
TT820 .C
746.43'4—dc22
2006025931

Printed in the United States of America

Design by Laura Palese
Photography by Henry Lopez
Technical editing and illustrations by Karen Manthey

10 9 8 7 6 5 4 3 2

First Edition

FOREWORD

"It gets a little complicated"—that's what I hear time and again about my designs. The leap from a pretty crocheted lace doily to an amazing, seamless lace garment is considerable. Therefore, this is not a learn-to-crochet book. To make the stuff in here you will need some crochet skills, if only the basics.

Mercifully, you won't actually have to read this book all the way through; some of it is necessarily technical. Many of the patterns are very long. In order to offer multiple sizing for certain designs, there had to be way more words. Sorry!

If it makes you happy to just look at the pictures and cool diagrams, feel free. But if you do decide to crochet something, please read my introduction. It explains my approach to seamless construction and presents a technique for making a foundation chain that is used in virtually every design in this book. If you find that this alternate foundation is unfamiliar to you, then please take the time to learn it. It's a little stitch that you will be happy to add to your bag of crochet tricks.

Thank you so much for being here.

ACKNOWLEDGMENTS

Hi, Mom! Hi, Harry! Hi, Nick! (Had to get that in right away.)

The writing of this crochet book has been a cathartic, therapeutic experience for me and a nice alternative to institutionalization. I wish to thank the following crochet therapists for their forbearance and advice in times of crisis:

Karen Manthey, my left-brain, technical editor, illustrator, conjurer of cool diagrams and schematics, miracle-worker.

Tammy Hildebrand, who without hesitation put her own designs on hold in order to slave over crochet samples for this book.

Susan Haviland, to whom I have a hard time saying "no," and all the Ladies at Lion Brand Yarn. Sorry about the mess.

The Ladies of the Riviera at Concord Stitch and Chat, who didn't giggle (much) when trying on my samples and didn't scold (much) about the missed meetings.

My friends from CGOA, pretty much all 2,000-plus members, but in particular my "musketeers," Vashti Braha, Marty Miller, and the aforementioned Tammy and Diane Moyer. Crochet ROCKS!

Nancy Thomas, who may yet be sweetly unaware that she has been to me a mentor and sounding-board.

For taking a chance on an untried author, to editor Rosy Ngo, and an amazing phalanx of editors and associates with myriad titles, including Shawna Mullen, Elizabeth Wright, Christina Schoen, Lauren Monchik, Amy Sly, and anyone and everyone at Potter Craft and Random House who had anything to do with the production of this book. Even if we've never met, I offer you my heartfelt gratitude.

I salute Sally Melville. As a result of not sleeping through her galvanizing lecture on creativity, I learned to write this book in my sleep!

I wish to acknowledge the following yarn companies and my contacts there for generously providing materials, with plenty of leftovers for my stash:

Susan Haviland, *Lion Brand Yarn* | Stacy Charles, *Tahki Stacy Charles* | Jonelle Raffino, *South West Trading Company* | Kathy Lacher, formerly at *Classic Elite* | Doris Erb, *Patons* | Norah Gaughan, *Berroco* | Kathleen Sams and Terri Geck, *Coats & Clark* | Uyvonne Bigham, *A2Z (Lily Chin Signature Collection)*

And I thank my loving and patient pack, John and Cookie, who now have a greater appreciation of home-cooked meals and clean laundry.

TABLE OF CONTENTS

TRIMMING ME

To understand my relationship with crochet and lace is to know the story of my mother. Jiu Lee Chan, née Pan, was born and raised in Yokohama, Japan, of ethnically Chinese parents. My grandfather was a happy-go-lucky, gregarious businessman in Yokohama's bustling Chinatown. My grandmother was a tiny, rather stern force of nature, a keeper of old traditions and superstitions. I met my grandparents only once, and all I can remember is staring and staring at my grandmother's bound feet and trying on her silk brocaded slippers, which were inches too small for my seven-year-old feet.

Among her four siblings, Mom did not receive much formal schooling. She stayed at home and trained in needlework, flower arranging, and dressmaking, all appropriate avocations for young women of her era and upbringing.

In 1954, as the bride of a Chinese-American U.S. Army serviceman and mother of a baby girl (me), she came to Fort Dix, New Jersey, where my father was stationed, bringing along with her a small trunk full of Chinese dresses, knitwear, crocheted doilies, and embellished handkerchiefs and linens, all the work of her own hands and those of her mother and sisters.

Otherwise, we didn't have much. Those early years were hard for my mom, not speaking the language or knowing the customs. It makes me cry to think how lonely, homesick, and isolated she was. Her entire world was my dad, the apartment, and little Doris. You have to give my mother credit, because she made the spartan army housing unit as pretty as possible. She decorated just about every surface with her handiwork. And she decorated me with the same enthusiasm.

Fate would have it that my mother yearned to raise a girly-girl. Mom loved to make ruffle-and-lace baby dresses with matching bows. The moment I grew enough hair, she began sticking those bows on my head. I have much photographic evidence to support this. My mother enjoys telling everyone how annoying I was, tearing off her beautiful doo-dads immediately after the shutter snapped, occasionally before the snap, or, as captured here during the shoot.

Glamour photo of Jiu Lee Pan, my mother, Yokohama, Japan, circa 1953.

Mom had to ease up on the bow thing because very soon my parents had two newer kids, my brothers, and a business to run. After his discharge from the army, my dad started a laundry. For a few years we lived in two tiny rooms at the back of the store. My mother had no time for doilies, what with caring for a growing family and laboring sixteen-hour days side by side with my dad.

1955, Army housing. See doily. See me in one of my earliest attempts at bow–removal. What matters a handful of hair?

In 1960, when the laundry earned enough so my parents could afford a house, the doilies came out of storage in a flurry of nesting. Anything that did not move was covered with lace and trim. After we all started school, Mom had a bit more time for herself and picked up her yarn work. She tried to teach me, starting with traditional crocheted granny squares and simple garter-stitch knit scarves. I sat still long enough to crochet bridles and saddle blankets for my toy horses, but none of that girly-girl stuff, and certainly none of that awful crochet doily stuff. Never.

That's why it is now so screamingly funny to my mother that I am crocheting, designing crochet, and writing a book full of crocheted lace. How's that for a big fat "See, I told you so!" My mother didn't read or follow patterns; she copied stitches and techniques by example from her mother, sisters, and teachers. I hardly expected her to remember enough to teach me now, nearly fifty years later. So much lovely work was lost through neglect or simply thrown out when worn and stained, so much I regret not appreciating when I had the chance. But I am getting ahead of the story.

I am convinced that my mother secretly wished that I'd had at least one girl, so she could try raising a girly granddaughter, but no dice. Wouldn't you know neither of my sons appreciated our bounty of adorable crocheted wear? Baby Harry would not keep

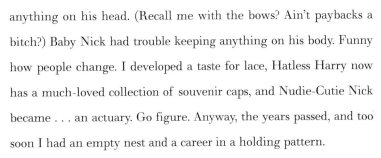

anything on his head. (Recall me with the bows? Ain't paybacks a bitch?) Baby Nick had trouble keeping anything on his body. Funny how people change. I developed a taste for lace, Hatless Harry now has a much-loved collection of souvenir caps, and Nudie-Cutie Nick became . . . an actuary. Go figure. Anyway, the years passed, and too soon I had an empty nest and a career in a holding pattern.

Mom's only surviving vintage thread doily.

My mom had never been in a local yarn shop or petted luxury yarns and, as a kid, I therefore never had either. With time on my hands I decided to give crochet another go, but only if I could take it to the next level. So I struck out on my own to encounter skills, tools, and yarns my mother never dreamed of. Self-improvement is a worthwhile destination, but trust me, it's a long and perilous journey.

In my wanderings I came across the thread crochet books of living legend Rita Weiss (she insists on that title herself). Something about those designs, the intricate patterns in stark white thread, caught my interest. They reminded me of Mom's doilies, the ones I grew up trashing. Now, to my mature eyes, they were awesome. I had no intention of working in thread. But something I read in the first page of Rita's book, *101 Crochet Edgings* (American School of Needlework, 1995), ignited a spark.

Rita wrote, "When choosing the thread and hook for your project, you may wish to do some experimenting with a variety of threads until you achieve the appearance and texture that pleases you." The more I thought about it, the more I could see taking Rita's words to the illogical extreme. What fun it would be to make these gorgeous lace designs, but really, really big. At that moment the "exploded" lace theory came into being.

Making garments with thick yarn and gigantic hooks was fun, but at first it was not easy. It took plenty of tinkering before I could figure out the perfect mating of yarn and hook, the best way to shape various stitch patterns. Each success taught me something, but each failure taught me even more.

When Dad died in 1997, Mom was lost, perhaps more lonely, homesick, and isolated than she had been when she first arrived here nearly fifty years before. She retired and traveled to Japan to see her sisters, but came back empty and forlorn. I wanted to draw her into my own newfound passion for crochet. Mom no longer had the desire to adorn me or fuss with thread crochet, no longer remembered any of those complicated patterns and stitches. Mom needed some instant gratification, simple handwork to take her mind off her grief, new and engaging projects she could do herself, could afford any time she wanted, and could wear with abandon.

Nothing captured her interest until, bursting with pride, I showed my mother the first crochet design I ever sold, the original exploded doily shawl. She admired it so much I was compelled to give her the one off my back. The next visit I made her try on one of my hats, a raccoon cap complete with striped tail. Turnaround time—now I was putting doo-dads on *her* head, but, unlike me at an earlier age, she liked it. Admittedly, that hat was kind of goofy, but she remarked that it was probably nice and warm. I was about to offer to make one for her, but on second thought, decided to show her how to make it herself. (Remember, she does not read patterns.) She had a difficult time with the fur-type yarns, used double stranded. But once she got the hang of feeling the stitches rather than seeing them, she took right to it. However, she refused to make the silly tail. Everyone's a critic.

Mom wore that hat and got so many compliments that she went out, bought a load of yarn, and stitched up dozens. That reconnection with her crochet helped pull my mom through a long stretch of depression after the loss of my dad and brought us even closer together. With yarn and hook in hand, there is no language barrier, no generation or cultural gap, no time, no worries. I can no longer imagine life without crochet. So it is with enormous gratitude and love that I dedicate this book to my first teacher, my worst critic, my best customer: my mother.

INTRODUCTION | my modus operandi

the theory of "exploded" lace

Generations of crocheters have worked these same stitches into their decorative items. What I do is make the lace patterns bigger, bolder, and more contemporary. It is a theory and a practice I call *exploded lace*.

What makes lace so interesting is the pictures we see in it, the conclusions our brains draw when we observe the solid parts (the stitches) juxtaposed against the empty space (the holes formed by the stitches). Some lace stitches combine to make us see shapes like flowers and leaves; some don't make a big picture but rather suggest geometry, symmetry, and balance between the there and the not-there.

Exploding is what happens when you crochet with thick yarns instead of fine thread, using oversized instead of steel hooks. The thicker the yarn, the bigger the hook, the more relaxed the gauge, the bolder the pictures you can produce. Astonishing but true: With the same effort and basic skills it takes to make a little doily in thread crochet, you can make . . . clothes! *Crocheted fashion* is no longer an oxymoron.

the stitch continuum

So how do you work with exploded crochet? The thread designs that serve as my inspiration are mainly small decorative items meant to lie flat. You can simply explode the original and have a large decorative item that can be draped around the body. A round doily becomes the round Chrysanthemum Tea Shawl (see page 22). But that's not all.

By ingenious manipulation of the stitches, we can shape more complex garments that fit human bodies. Unfortunately, the same qualities that make exploded lace so cool—big, bold patterns and loose, malleable, free-breathing fabric—also make it a bitch to shape and sew together.

Seaming crochet has always been problematic for me. Aside from decorative applications where they are meant to stand out, my crocheted seams are clumsy and ugly. The side edges (row-ends) never match up, particularly with fancy lace patterns. For me, the fewer seams the better.

From playing around with doily and afghan motifs, I learned joining as you go.

Each motif is crocheted up to the last round, then crocheted onto the previous motif while making the last round. It is often more complicated than you'd think, but it's no-sew and allows the lace pattern to continue from piece to piece.

I also began to understand how doily circles and squares are shaped into larger and larger rounds by increasing within the stitch patterns, "growing" them if you will, in a calculable way. The yoke of a sweater is just a giant motif, somewhere between a circle and a square, with controlled pattern growth at four "raglan" points. Since most doilies are made from the center out, I naturally gravitated toward making my exploded doily garments from the neck down. Through trial and error I figured out how to take a pretty stitch pattern and grow an exploded, shoulder-shaped motif. Once I adopted a "join as you go" attitude about the rest of the parts, my chief MO was born.

Freed from the confines of precise, rigid seaming, the exploded lace fabric can mold, drape, and breathe; the lace patterns can wrap around the body uncorrupted and uninterrupted. I stumbled upon the secrets of how to coax balls of yarn to grow, seamlessly, into beautiful garments that look nice on the body, the joy of which I mean to share with you in this book.

foundation and crochet

Every piece of crocheted fabric begins with the most basic stitch, the chain. Usually a specific number of chains are made for a foundation chain, upon which is built the first row or round of stitches. Working into the foundation chain is the most irritating, frustrating, tedious (expletive deleted!) part of crochet, and I know I am not alone in making this allegation. Many beginner crocheters are totally discouraged by this fundamental step, throw up their hands in surrender, and run screaming, never to return. Teachers often have to make the foundation chain and first row for their students, particularly young ones, just so they can move on to the good stuff.

The traditional chain foundation has other problems:

counting. Who the heck wants to count and then stitch into dozens, perhaps hundreds of chains? Every crocheter has tips for working with long chains. You can always make extra chains and then un-chain the unused ones later. You can place markers every 20 or 50 or whatever number of chains to help you keep count. Handy, but still not fun.

gauge. Very few crocheters make the chain stitch at the same gauge as the rest of the stitches. It is natural and typical to chain tighter. That's why so many patterns admonish you to make the foundation chain loose, in order to compensate for that.

lack of elasticity. A chain foundation does not allow much stretch or give, properties you would like to have in, say, a neckline or a waistline.

sagging and gapping. Particularly in a neckline that will be finished with a collar or some kind of trim, chain foundations get pulled horribly out of shape by the weight of the rest of the garment, leaving huge, unacceptable gaps.

There is no way around the foundation. However, there are better foundations. The following alternate method, which in this book is called "base chain single crochet," or BASE CH/SC, is similar to other no-chain techniques such as Bill Elmore's double-faced foundation. Think of it as piggybacking. You begin with a short chain, make a stitch in that chain, then make the next stitch into the bottom of the first stitch, and so on. The top edge and bottom edge look much the same and are equally easy to crochet upon later.

My variation of choice creates a foundation chain and a single crochet in one that simply and elegantly addresses all of the problems I was having with the traditional chain foundation. It also works well in tandem with my MO. Compared to the traditional chain, it is sturdier, more elastic, and a piece of pie to count. You never have to work into another long chain. That in itself is reason enough to love this technique. Best of all for my exploded lace and top-down designs, it solves the problem of too-tight chains that choke up or too-loose chains that sag and gap.

The exact method I use is subtly different from the versions I've seen illustrated in stitch guides. So here's the BASE CH/SC, step by step. I ask you to learn this foundation before making any of the designs in this book. If you are unfamiliar with the technique, I suggest a bit of practice. After you get used to it, it goes fast and you will love it.

NOTE: Here is how I work into a chain. It is not the only way, nor is it always the best way, but for your information that's the way it is worked in this book. A chain has two faces. The front face looks like a heart, or the two loops that form the top of other stitches. At the back of the chain is a bump or nub. Some crocheters insert the hook into the face of the chain, going under just one strand. Some insert the hook under the two strands of the face, under two loops, the way you work other stitches.

Some insert the hook under the nub at the back of the chain, under one loop only. I prefer to insert the hook into the front face of the chain AND under the nub at the back, under *two* loops.

the base ch/sc as a foundation

1st stitch:

Ch 2, insert hook into the 2nd ch from hook (into the front face of the chain AND under the nub at the back of the chain) under 2 lps (step 1 on page 14)/(see step 2 on page 14). YO and draw up a lp. There are 2 lps on hook. YO and draw through 2 lps on hook (step 3 on page 14).

That is just like making a normal single crochet into a chain. That sc has 2 lps that form the top of the stitch and strands that form the stem of the stitch.

2nd stitch:

Insert hook under 2 strands at the forward edge of the stem of the prev sc (step 4 on page 14). It will resemble the way you insert the hook into a chain. YO and draw up a lp. There are 2 lps on hook. YO and draw through one lp on hook (step 5 on page 14). You have just made the "chain" that lies along the base of the foundation. There are 2 lps on hook. YO and draw through 2 lps on hook (step 6 on page 14). You have just made the "sc."

3rd stitch:

Insert hook into the "chain" at the base of the stitch just made, into the front face AND under the back nub, under 2 strands (step 7 on page 14). YO and draw up a lp. There are 2 lps on hook. YO and draw through one lp on hook (step 8 on page 14). You have just made the "chain." YO and draw through 2 lps on hook (step 9 on page 14). You have just made the "sc."

Make the rem BASE CH/SC same as 3rd stitch, except the last.

last stitch:

Insert hook into the "chain," under 2 strands. YO and draw up a lp, YO and draw through 2 lps on hook.

NOTE: Notice that the 1st and last BASE CH/SC stitches are missing a step and thus are a bit shorter than the others. I like to compress the ends of this foundation. It keeps the ends neater when you work your first row of stitches.

BASE CH/SC

step 1:

ch 2, insert hook in 2nd ch from hook.

step 2:

YO, draw yarn through st.

step 3:

YO, draw yarn through 2 lps on hook.

step 4:

First sc made. Insert hook under 2 strands at the forward edge of previous sc.

step 5:

YO, draw up a lp (2 lps on hook), YO, draw through 1 lp on hook for ch.

step 6:

Ch made (2 lps on hook). YO, draw through 2 lps on hook.

step 7: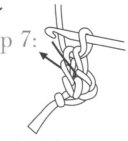

Second sc made. Insert hook under the first 2 strands of the ch at the base of last sc.

step 8: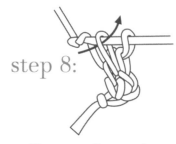

YO, draw up a lp (2 lps on hook), YO, draw through 1 lp on hook for ch.

step 9:

Ch made (2 lps on hook). YO, draw through 2 lps on hook.

step 10:

Third sc made.

Repeat steps 7–10 for desired length of foundation chain.

the base ch/sc as a ring

Same as a flat foundation, except make the last stitch the same as the 3rd stitch. Being careful not to twist the stitches, sl st by inserting the hook into the 1st sc, under the 2 lps at the top of the stitch just as you would for a normal sc. YO and complete sl st.

NOTE: There will be some extra height, a "jog" where the ring is joined together. You have joined the ring at the "sc." You need to go back and join the ring at the "ch." To make a neat finish there, take the tail end, thread it onto a yarn needle if that makes it easier and weave it around the "ch" at the base of the last stitch in the ring and back into the beg ch.

the base ch/sc as an add-on

The BASE CH/SC is also useful for adding stitches at the end of a row or when joining the underarm of a seamless garment. You can make a BASE CH/SC after completing any stitch. The stitch just made before the BASE CH/SC (a single crochet, double crochet, triple crochet, or whatever) will always have two loops at the top of the stitch, the ones you would normally work under. Just below that, there are strands that form the "stem." Whatever the stitch, you will begin the BASE CH/SC by inserting the hook under two strands of the forward edge of the stem of the stitch just made, closest to the top loops of the stitch. I always call for a "ch 1" to begin, so as not to compress the end.

Ch 1, insert hook under 2 strands of the forward edge of stem of prev st, YO and draw up a lp, YO and draw through 2 lps. Make rem sts same as 3rd stitch above. Continue with work.

working into the base ch/sc

Turn the foundation so the loops of the "sc" are on top. Work the first row of pattern stitches into those sc, under the top 2 loops, the same way you would work normal stitches.

The "ch" edge looks fairly neat and is an acceptable edge as is for a piece. However, I sometimes work a finishing row or round. What is left over along the "ch" edge is a bit different from either a chain or a stitch. There's the top of the stitch, two strands that resemble the top loops of a normal stitch, and there is a funny third strand beneath or beside that. You may work into any of the strands or any combination of the strands you wish. It doesn't really matter, as long as you are consistent. I mostly work under all the spare strands, particularly when working parts of the foundation that already have stitches in them on the other side. Occasionally, when the yarn is really thick, I will work under the top two strands of the "ch" edge, leaving the funny third strand. The result is a line across the foundation where that strand is left unworked, but it is not unattractive.

approaching the mo

Here are a few tips for working with the MO. Some may sound ridiculous or aggravating to do. Please persevere.

relax. These are oversized gauges, often looser than normally advised for the yarn. I've seen crocheters who wind the feeder yarn several times around their fingers and crochet so tightly they have a difficult time inserting the hook into their stitches. Your goal is to make relaxed, drapey fabric, not potholders.

give it a fair chance. Allow yourself a big slice of quality time when beginning a project with new yarns, construction techniques, and stitches. Give your complete attention to the starting and establishing of the stitch pattern. Many crocheters have told me that once you get the yarn in your hands and go stitch by stitch, you get the hang of it. Stock plenty of analgesics just in case.

the gauge swatch. This is going to sound very wrong, contradictory to everything they tell you about crochet. The usual square swatch, incorporating the yarn, hook, and a few reps and rows of stitch pattern, may prove impossible to configure, given the idiosyncratic nature of the MO. Don't even bother to go there. I will get a lot of argument over that last bit. Please read on.

Anything with motifs may be swatched by making the first rounds of a motif, but with the shaped garments, this is asking for a leap of faith...

Jump right in. Use the hook I used and make the foundation, a base chain single crochet (BASE CH/SC), to the approximate measurement given. That is the first indication of whether you are in the ballpark. Do not hesitate to change hook sizes. Assuming that your foundation is close enough, go ahead and work the first few rows or rounds.

You'll notice when setting up the first row that the pattern may be squeezed on, with more stitches and reps across the foundation than it needs. This is calculated to increase the piece right away and give the top of shoulder immediate ease. You need to complete enough rows and give the pattern a chance to breathe before you can get an accurate gauge measurement. Admittedly, that's quite a bit of the project, a few inches, which means you could have a lot of deconstruction if your gauge is not close enough. But didn't we all get that memo? Crochet means frequently having to "un" crochet.

measure. Do it where there's a big enough patch of unshaped, straight-ahead stitch pattern, usually at the middle of the back. Give the piece a good tug in all directions. Smooth it out, allow it to spring back if it wants to, and then measure.

Even while you are crocheting at the exact stated gauge, don't be alarmed if your piece seems out of proportion, in particular if it seems too short. It has been my experience that certain yarns and open lace stitches will grow after working the entire length of the garment, after blocking, and then again after hanging and wearing.

mark everything. My pattern pages resemble road maps when I'm done. Check off rows as you complete them. Mark repeated phrases or pattern rows for easy viewing. Place markers in your crochet as well. You can use the "scrap of contrasting yarn" method, but these can and do fall out. Split ring markers are great and widely available. I get cocky on occasion and forgo marking my own work, trusting instead my vast experience (ha!) with this MO. I don't want to tell you how many times I have put corners in the wrong place . . . or made too many corners.

check your work. This does not mean you have to stop and count everything. Glance back every few reps to see if the pattern is chugging along nicely. And take the opportunity at the end of each row or round to inspect the one you just made. This is the one rule I ignore all the time in my excitement at seeing the lace develop. But man, you want to beat yourself upside the head when you've worked a huge long round of a doily pattern and find a fatal error in the previous round.

loose ends. The inside of your garment should look (almost) as beautiful as the outside, and that means dealing with loose ends. With this MO there's no place to hide them. Try to join yarn in the most inconspicuous place possible, at the end of a row or at the side of a round, while in the process of making a tall stitch, like a double or triple crochet. Later, thread each end on the thinnest yarn needle you can manage and weave it down and back up the tall stitch.

block. Always block lace. Use the measurements given in the schematic as a guideline. I wet-blocked practically everything in this book. Other methods work just as well, such as damp blocking or steaming, so do whatever works for you.

I block garments as I would wear them, layering fronts on top of backs, arms angled out to the sides, giving them a body shape. Ease the piece into the shape and size you want and open up the lace pattern. You can compensate for some of the vagaries of gauge and stitch at this point.

View the garment from different angles to check the proportions. You can tweak some of the details. Make the edges edgier, the curves curvier, the points pointier. Admire your work. This is probably the first time you're seeing the stitch pattern "pop." Wow! I made this! Compel your loved ones to come and see the beauty. Savor the moment. Allow the piece to dry completely.

about those diagrams

Crochet diagrams are a handy visual way to convey a crochet pattern. Each stitch is represented by a symbol as shown in the stitch key below. Special stitches, such as clusters and shells, use a combination of these same stitches.

When a pattern is worked in rows, right-side rows are worked from right to left; wrong-side rows go from left to right. A row number usually shows where the row begins. When no row numbers are given, look for the beginning chain. Circular pieces are read counterclockwise on right-side rows and clockwise on wrong-side rows. Whenever possible, an entire pattern is drawn out. For complex patterns, a sample of the basic pattern stitch may be provided. For larger pieces, a section of the pattern that includes one or more repeats may be shown.

abbreviations and symbols

Crochet skill level symbols and ballband symbols for yarn weight are the standardized systems created by the Craft Yarn Council of America.

See and download a complete handbook of Yarn Standards and Guidelines from the CYCA sponsored website, www.yarnstandards.com.

Abbreviations for special stitches or stitch combinations are explained in each pattern.

standard yarn weight system

SUPER FINE
Sock, Fingering, Baby

FINE
Sport, Baby

LIGHT
DK, Light Worsted

MEDIUM
Worsted, Afghan, Aran

BULKY
Chunky, Craft, Rug

SUPER BULKY
Bulky, Roving

When describing yarn as "bulky" or "sportweight," different people mean different things. The Craft Yarn Council of America has established guidelines called the Standard Yarn Weight System to standardize descriptions of yarn thickness. The materials section of each pattern in this book features an icon of a skein of yarn with a number on it. That number corresponds to one of these categories. The guiding principle of this system is the smaller the number, the thinner the yarn.

stitch key

- • = slip stitch (sl st)

- � = chain (ch)

- ✕ = single crochet (sc)

- ┬ = half double crochet (hdc)

- ┬ = double crochet (dc)

- ┬ = treble crochet (tr)

- ┬ = double treble crochet (dtr)

abbreviations

Here is a list of common abbreviations I've used throughout.

approx	approximate, approximately	prev	previous
beg	begin, beginning	rem	remain, remaining
bet	between	rep(s)	repeat, repeats
ch	chain, chain stitch	rev sc	reverse single crochet
ch-	refers to a chain or space previously made	rnd(s)	round, rounds
ch-sp	chain space	RS	right side
CL	cluster	sc	single crochet
cont	continue, continues, continuing	sc2tog	single crochet two together
dc	double crochet	sk	skip
dc2tog	double crochet two stitches together	sl st	slip stitch
dec	decrease, decreases, decreasing	sp(s)	space, spaces
dtr	double triple crochet	st(s)	stitch, stitches
foll	follow, follows, following	tch	turning chain
FP	front post	tbl	through back loop
hdc	half double crochet	tfl	through front loop
inc	increase, increases, increasing	tog	together
lp(s)	loop, loops	tr	triple or treble crochet
patt	pattern, patterns	WS	wrong side
		yo	yarn over

special stitches

 = front post double crochet (FPdc)

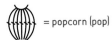 = back post double crochet (BPdc)

 = popcorn (pop)

 = examples of shells

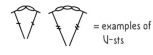 = examples of V-sts

 = examples of clusters (CL)

 = example of a fan

chapter one | GARDEN PARTY |

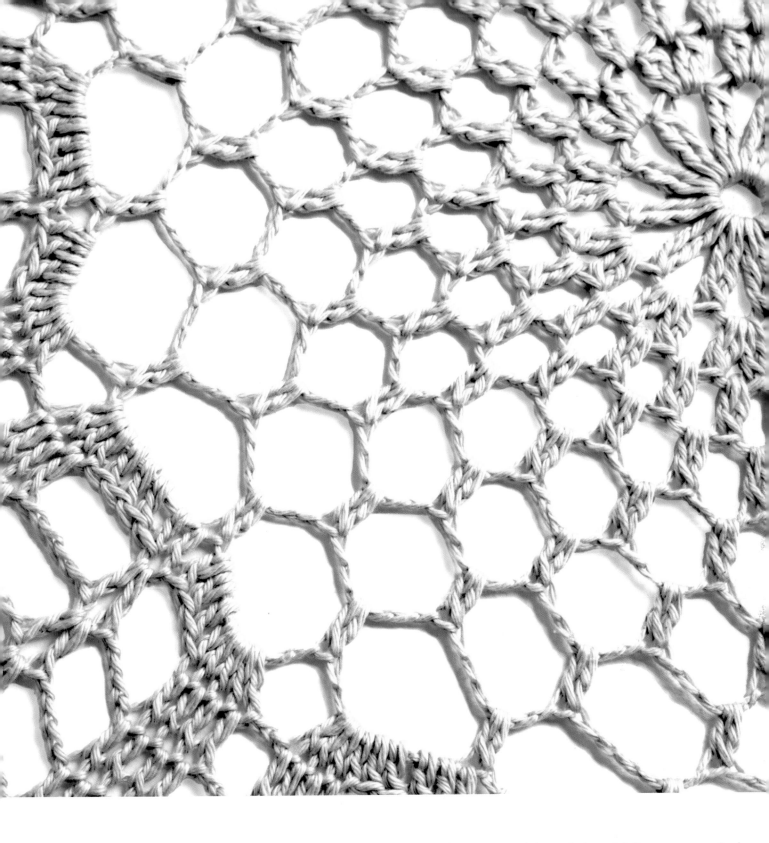

chrysanthemum tea shawl

Here is the quintessential translation of doily to garment. I adapted stitch patterns from three different doilies, vintage and new, and put them into this round exploded doily shawl. The yarn is a modern blend of cotton and Tencel, with a slight sheen, soft silky hand, and great stitch definition. To wear, fold over about a third of the circle and arrange the fold as a collar high on the neck. The ruffles that drape gracefully over the shoulders and across the back give "garden party" charm to any outfit.

size

One size fits most

Approx 48" (122cm) in diameter

materials

Classic Elite "Premiere"; 50% Pima cotton, 50% Tencel; 1 3/4 oz (50g)/108 yd (99m)

7 hanks in #5235 (light green)

Size I-9 (5.5mm) crochet hook or size needed to obtain gauge

Yarn needle

gauge

In patt, Rnds 1–3 = 6" (15cm) in diameter. Not critical, but keep work relaxed to achieve size.

SPECIAL STITCHES

dc2tog: (YO, insert hook in next st, YO, draw yarn through st, YO, draw yarn through 2 lps on hook) twice, YO, draw yarn through 3 lps on hook.

dc3tog: (YO, insert hook in next st, YO, draw yarn through st, YO, draw yarn through 2 lps on hook) 3 times, YO, draw yarn through 4 lps on hook.

dc4tog: (YO, insert hook in next st, YO, draw yarn through st, YO, draw yarn through 2 lps on hook) 4 times, YO, draw yarn through 5 lps on hook.

tr2tog: (YO [twice], insert hook in next ch-sp, YO, draw yarn through ch-sp, [YO, draw yarn through 2 lps on hook] twice) twice in same ch-sp, YO, draw yarn through 4 lps on hook.

tr3tog: (YO [twice], insert hook in next ch-sp, YO, draw yarn through ch-sp, [YO, draw yarn through 2 lps on hook] twice) 3 times in same ch-sp, YO, draw yarn through 4 lps on hook.

CL (dc cluster): dc2tog in same st or sp.

V-st: (dc, ch 2, dc) in same st or sp.

V in V: (dc, ch 2, dc) in ch-2 sp of next V-st.

INSTRUCTIONS

NOTE: This design is worked from the center out in joined rounds, with the RS always facing, as is traditional for round doilies. Keep your work, particularly your chains, relaxed for the airiest effect.

Ch 8, sl st in beg ch to form a ring.

RND 1: Ch 3, tr in ring, (ch 2, tr2tog) 11 times in ring, ch 1, sc in top of beg ch: 12 ch-sps.

RND 2: Ch 2, dc in first sp, ch 1, (CL, ch 1, CL, ch 1) in each of next 11 ch-sps, CL in same sp as beg, sc in top of beg ch: 24 ch-sps.

RND 3: Ch 2, dc in first sp, ch 2, (CL, ch 2) in each of next 23 ch-sps, ending with ch 1, sc in top of beg ch: 24 ch-sps.

RND 4: Ch 2, dc in first sp, ch 3, (CL, ch 3) in each ch-sp around, ending with ch 1, hdc in top of beg ch.

RND 5: Ch 2, dc in first sp, ch 4, (CL, ch 4) in each ch-sp around, ending with ch 1, dc in top of beg ch.

RND 6: Ch 2, dc in first sp, ch 5, (CL, ch 5) in each ch-sp around, ending with ch 2, dc in top of beg ch.

RND 7: Ch 2, dc in first sp, ch 6, (CL, ch 6) in each ch-sp around, ending with ch 3, dc in top of beg ch.

RND 8: Ch 2, dc in first sp, ch 7, (CL, ch 7) in

each ch-sp around, sl st in top of beg ch.

RND 9: Sl st in first ch-sp, ch 3, 7 dc in same sp, *dc in next dc, 8 dc in next ch-sp, ch 2, 8 dc in next ch-sp; rep from * around, except omit last 8 dc, instead sl st in top of beg ch: 12 leaf reps.

RND 10: Ch 3, dc in next 3 dc, *ch 4, skip next 3 dc, V-st in next dc, ch 4, sk next 3 dc, ch 2, dc in next 4 dc; rep from * around, except omit last 4 dc, instead sl st in top of beg ch.

RND 11: Ch 3, dc in next 3 dc, *ch 4, sk next ch-4 sp, V in V, ch 4, sk next ch-4 sp, dc in next 4 dc, ch 3, dc in next 4 dc; rep from * around, except omit last 4 dc, instead sl st in top of beg ch.

RND 12: Ch 3, dc in next 3 dc, *ch 4, sk next ch-4 sp, V in V, ch 4, sk next ch-4 sp, dc in next 4 dc, ch 4, dc in next 4 dc; rep from * around, except omit last 4 dc, instead sl st in top of beg ch.

RND 13: Ch 3, dc in next 3 dc, *ch 4, sk next ch-4 sp, V in V, ch 4, sk next ch-4 sp, dc in next 4 dc, ch 5, dc in next 4 dc; rep from * around, except omit last 4 dc, instead sl st in top of beg ch.

RND 14: Ch 3, dc in next 3 dc, *ch 4, sk next ch-4 sp, V in V, ch 4, sk next ch-4 sp, dc in next 4 dc, ch 6, dc in next 4 dc; rep from * around, except omit last 4 dc, instead sl st in top of beg ch.

RND 15: Ch 3, dc in next 3 dc, *ch 3, sk next ch-4 sp, V in V, ch 3, sk next ch-4 sp, dc in next 4 dc, ch 4, CL in next ch-sp, ch 4, dc in next 4 dc; rep from * around, except omit last 4 dc, instead sl st in top of beg ch.

RND 16: Ch 3, dc in next 3 dc, *ch 2, sk next ch-3 sp, V in V, ch 2, sk next ch-3 sp, dc in next 4 dc, ch 5, CL in next ch-sp, ch 3, CL in next ch-sp, ch 5, dc in next 4 dc; rep from * around, except omit last 4 dc, instead sl st in top of beg ch.

RND 17: Ch 3, dc in next 3 dc, *ch 1, sk next ch-2 sp, V in V, ch 1, sk next ch-2 sp, dc in next 4 dc, ch 5, (CL, ch 3) in each of next 2 ch-sps, CL in next ch-sp, ch 5, dc in next 4 dc; rep from * around, except omit last 4 dc, instead sl st in top of beg ch.

RND 18: Ch 3, dc in next 3 dc, *ch 3, sk next ch-1 sp, sc in ch-2 sp of next V, ch 3, sk next ch-1 sp, dc in next 4 dc, ch 5, (CL, ch 3) in each of next 3 ch-sps, CL in next ch-sp, ch 5, dc in next 4 dc; rep from * around, except omit last 4 dc, instead sl st in top of beg ch.

RND 19: Ch 3, dc in next 3 dc, *ch 2, dc in next 4 dc, ch 5, (CL, ch 3) in each of next 4 ch-sps, CL in next ch-sp, ch 5, dc in next 4 dc; rep from * around, except omit last 4 dc, instead sl st in top of beg ch.

RND 20: Ch 3, dc in next 3 dc, *sk next ch-2 sp, dc in next 4 dc, ch 5, (CL, ch 3) in each of next 5 ch-sps, CL in next ch-sp, ch 5, dc in next 4 dc; rep from * around, except omit last 4 dc, instead sl st in top of beg ch.

RND 21: Ch 3, dc in next dc, *(dc2tog in next 2 dc) twice, dc in next 2 dc, ch 5, (CL, ch 3) in each of next 6 ch-sps, CL in next ch-sp, ch 5, dc in next 2 dc; rep from * around, except omit last 2 dc, instead sl st in top of beg ch.

RND 22: Ch 3, *(dc2tog in next 2 dc) twice, dc in next dc, ch 5, (CL, ch 3) in each of next 7 ch-sps, CL in next ch-sp, ch 5, dc in next dc; rep from * around, except omit last dc, instead sl st in top of beg ch.

RND 23: Ch 2, dc3tog in next 3 dc, *ch 5, (CL, ch 3) in each of next 8 ch-sps, CL in next ch-sp, ch 5, dc4tog in next 4 dc; rep from * around, except omit last ch 5 and dc4tog, instead ch 2, dc in top of beg ch: 12 dc4tog.

RND 24: Ch 2, dc in first sp, (ch 3, CL in next ch-sp) 119 times, ch 1, hdc in top of beg ch: 120 ch-3 sps.

RND 25: Ch 1, sc in first sp, *(tr3tog, ch 3, tr3tog, ch 3, tr3tog) in next ch-sp (shell made), sc in next ch-sp, ch 5, sc in next ch-sp; rep from * around, except omit last ch 5 and sc, instead ch 2, dc in top of beg sc: 40 shells.

RND 26: Ch 1, sc in first sp, ch 5, (sc, ch 5) in each ch-sp around, sl st in beg sc: 120 ch-5 sps.

RND 27: Sl st in next ch-sp, ch 1, 7 sc in each ch-sp around, sl st in beg sc: 840 sc. Fasten off. Weave ends. Block shawl to 48" (122cm) in diameter.

Chrysanthemum Tea Shawl Diagram

flower power vest

A floral motif borrowed from a lace table runner is easily adapted into this adorable, quick-to-crochet design. Two exploded flowers are attached with extra mesh for straps and sides to form a scoop-neck, cropped vest. The multicolored, springy ribbon yarn is wonderful for this kind of oversized gauge. It's the star of this vest, even more than the fancy stitch work!

size

Directions are given for size Small (S). Changes for Medium (M) and Large (L) are in parentheses. Sample is size Small.

Finished bust: 36 (40, 44)" (91.5 [101½, 112]cm).

Back length 18 (18, 19)" (46 [46, 48]cm).

NOTE: Vest is very stretchy.

materials

Moda Dea "Ticker Tape"; Art. R117; 100% nylon; 1¾ oz (50g); 67 yd (62m)

3 (4, 4) balls in #9263 Monet

Size N-15 (10mm) crochet hook

gauge

Rnds 1–3 of Motif = 7½" (19cm) in diameter; Motif = 16 x 16" (40.5 x 40.5cm) before assembly.

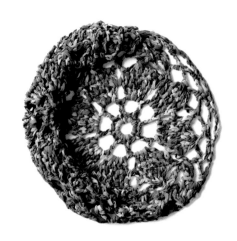

SPECIAL STITCHES

dc4tog: (YO, insert hook in next st, YO, draw yarn through st, YO, draw yarn through 2 lps on hook) 4 times, YO, draw yarn through all lps on hook.

dc5tog: (YO, insert hook in next st, YO, draw yarn through st, YO, draw yarn through 2 lps on hook) 5 times, YO, draw yarn through all lps on hook.

3-tr CL: (YO [twice], insert hook in next st, YO, draw yarn through st, YO, draw yarn through 2 lps on hook [twice]) 3 times in same st, YO, draw yarn through 4 lps on hook.

6-tr CL: 3 tr (half closed) in next ch-sp (4 lps on hook), 3 tr (half closed) in next ch-sp (7 lps on hook), YO, draw yarn through 7 lps on hook.

PICOT: Ch 5, sl st in top of last CL made.

INSTRUCTIONS

Make 2 Motifs, join with additional mesh for straps and sides.

motif (make 2)

Made in joined rnds, with RS always facing.

Ch 8, sl st in beg ch to form a ring.

RND 1: Ch 1, work 16 sc in ring, sl st in beg sc: 16 sc.

RND 2: Ch 7 (counts as dc, ch 4), sk beg sc, sk next sc, (dc in next sc, ch 4, sk next sc) 7 times, sl st in 3rd ch of beg ch: 8 ch-sps.

RND 3: Ch 3 (counts as dc), 4 dc in next ch-sp, ch 2, (5 dc, ch 2) in each of next 7 ch-sps, sl st in top of beg ch: 8 petals of 5 dc.

RND 4: Ch 3 (counts as dc), sk beg dc, dc in next 4 dc, *(dc, ch 3, dc) in next ch-sp, dc in each of next 5 dc; rep from * 6 times, (dc, ch 3, dc) in next ch-sp, sl st in top of beg ch.

RND 5: Ch 3 (counts as dc), sk beg dc, dc4tog in next 4 dc of first petal, *ch 5, sc in next ch-sp, ch 5, sk next dc, dc5tog worked across next 5 dc of petal; rep from * 6 times, ch 5, sc in next ch-sp, ch 2, dc in top of beg ch (to bring end of rnd to center of last ch-sp).

RND 6: Ch 1, sc in same sp, ch 5, sc in next ch-sp, ch 5, *3-tr CL in next sc for corner, ch 5, (sc, ch 5) in each of next 4 sps; rep from * twice, 3-tr CL in next sc for corner, (ch 5, sc) in each of next 2 in ch-sps, ch 2, dc in beg sc: 4 corners.

RND 7: Ch 1, sc in same sp, (ch 5, sc) in each of next 2 ch-sps, *ch 5, 6-tr CL worked over ch-sp to the right of corner and next ch-sp to the left of corner, PICOT, ch 5, sc in same ch-sp to left of corner**, (ch 5, sc) in each of next 4 ch-sps; rep from * twice; rep from * to ** once, ch 5, sc in next ch-sp, ch 5, sl st in beg sc. Fasten off. Weave ends.

SIZES SMALL AND MEDIUM ONLY
first strap
S/M ROW 1 (WS): With WS of one Motif facing, locate top right-hand corner picot, sk next 4 ch-5 sps, join yarn with sl st in next ch-5 sp, ch 5, sc in next ch-5 sp, ch-5, sc in next picot, turn.

S/M ROW 2: (Ch 5, sc in next ch-5 sp) twice, turn.

With WS of both Motifs facing, matching ch-5 sps and corner picot, work Row 3 to join Strap to 2nd Motif.

S/M ROW 3 (WS) (JOINING ROW): Ch 2, sl st in corresponding ch-5 sp of 2nd Motif (2nd ch-5 sp to the right of corner picot), ch 2, sc in next ch-5 sp of first Motif, ch 2, sl st in next ch-5 sp of 2nd Motif, ch 2, sc in next ch-5 sp of first Motif, ch 2, sl st in picot of 2nd Motif, ch 2, sl st in same ch-5 sp of first Motif.

Fasten off.

second strap
S/M ROW 1 (WS): With WS of 2nd Motif facing, sk 2 ch-5 sps to the left of last joined ch-sp of First Strap, join yarn with sl st in next ch-5 sp, ch 5, sc in next ch-5 sp, ch-5, sc in next picot, turn.

S/M ROWS 2–3: Rep ROWS 2–3 of First Strap, joining to corresponding sps on First Motif.

Fasten off. Weave ends.

SIZE LARGE ONLY
first strap
Size Large requires an additional row of mesh for Straps.

L ROW 1 (RS): With RS of one Motif facing, join yarn with sl st in top right-hand corner picot, ch 5, sc in next ch-5 sp, ch-5, sc in next ch-5 sp, turn.

L ROWS 2–3: (Ch 5, sc in next ch-5 sp) twice, turn.

L ROW 4 (WS) (JOINING ROW): Rep S/M ROW 3. Fasten off.

Weave ends.

second strap
L ROW 1 (WS): With RS of 2nd Motif facing, join yarn with sl st in top right-hand corner picot, ch 5, sc in next ch-5 sp, ch-5, sc in next ch-5 sp, turn.

L ROWS 2–4: Rep ROWS 2–4 of First Strap. Fasten off.

Weave ends.

ALL SIZES
left side panel
ROW 1: With RS of Front facing, working across left side edge, sk first ch-5 sp to the left of joined corner picot, join yarn with sl st in next ch-5 sp, (ch 5, sc) in each of next 4 ch-5 sps, ch 5, sc in next picot, turn: 5 ch-5 sps.

ROW 2: (Ch 5, sc) in each of next 5 ch-5 sps, turn: 5 ch-5 sps.

Rep ROW 2 (0 [2, 4] times).

With RS facing, holding two Motifs side by side, matching ch-5 sps and corner picot along right side edge of Back Motif and Side, work next row to join Left Side to Back edge.

ROW 3 (5, 7) (JOINING ROW): *Ch 2, sl st in corresponding ch-5 sp of 2nd Motif, ch 2, sc in next ch-5 sp of first Motif; rep from * 4 times, ch 2, sl st in picot of 2nd Motif, ch 2, sl st in same ch-5 sp of first Motif. Fasten off.

right side panel
ROW 1: With RS of Back facing, working across right side edge, sk first ch-5 sp to the left of joined corner picot, join yarn with sl st in next ch-5 sp, (ch 5, sc in next ch-5 sp) 4 times, ch 5, sc in next picot, turn: 5 ch-5 sps.

Complete same as Left Side Panel.

Weave ends, block vest.

BASIC MOTIF

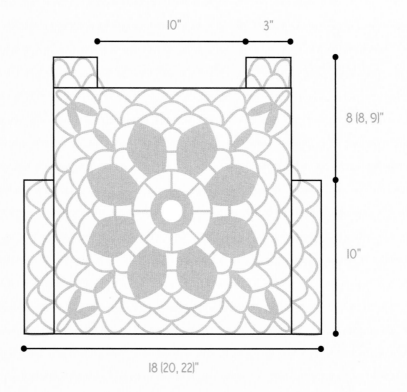

10"   3"

8 (8, 9)"

10"

18 (20, 22)"

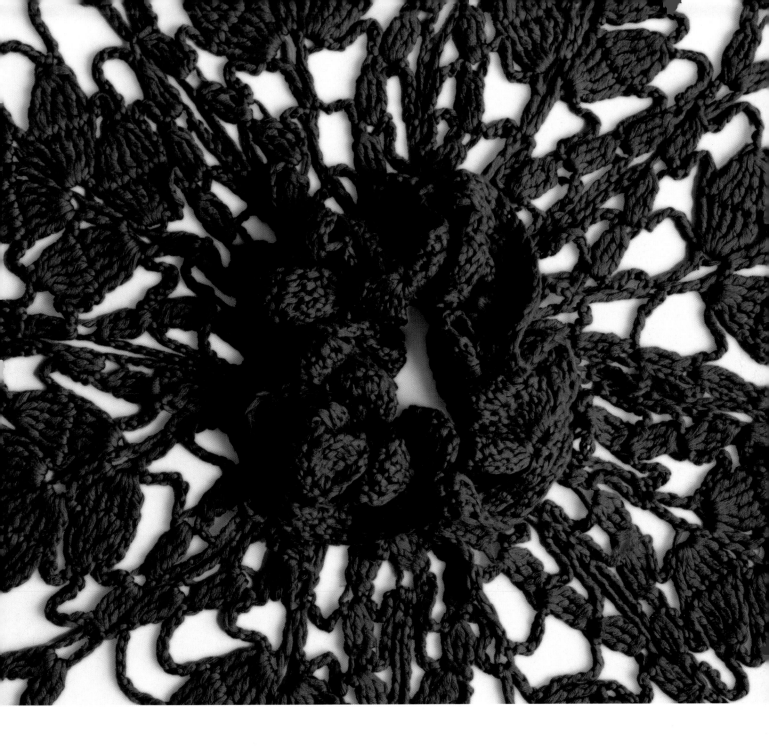

plum blossom capelet

Inspired by the "Flower and Fern Mat" pattern (from *McCall's Needlework Treasury*, first published in 1950), this capelet is an exploded round doily with the center part left out to make a hole for your head. It is crocheted in a super silky bamboo yarn with a soft finish—so soft that the lower edge needed more swing. Employing an easy beading technique, I tipped each of the fringe ends with a fire-polished glass bead. The beads aren't in your face; they just help the capelet hang as beautifully as it does, in the same manner as the weights that are sewn into the hems of draperies. (For more in-depth exploration of beading, see Lily Chin's book *Knit and Crochet With Beads.*)

size

One size fits most

Neck opening: 28" (71cm) in circumference

Bottom edge: 68" (173cm) in circumference

Finished length: 18" (46cm)

materials

Classic Elite "Bam Boo"; 100% bamboo; 1³/₄ oz (50g); 77 yd (70m)

6 balls in #4956 (purple)

Size J-10 (6mm) crochet hook

Fine steel crochet hook for beading technique

48 beads, amethyst

Sample shown uses 6 mm fire-polished glass beads, akin to pebble beads or small crow or pony beads.

gauge

12 BASE CH/SC of neck = 4" (10cm)

In patt, 2 rows CL or 2 rows leaf = 2" (5cm)

NOTE: Gauge is not super critical, but keep work relaxed to achieve length.

SPECIAL STITCHES

BASE CH/SC: See Introduction.

CL (cluster) (tr3tog in same st): (YO [twice], insert hook in st, YO, draw yarn through st [YO, draw yarn through 2 lps on hook] twice) 3 times in same st, YO, draw yarn through 4 lps on hook.

BEG CL (ch 4, tr2tog in same st) (begins all but one round): Ch 4, (YO [twice], insert hook in st, YO, draw yarn through st, [YO, draw yarn through 2 lps on hook] twice) twice in same st, YO, draw yarn through 4 lps on hook.

SHELL: 5 tr in same st or sp.

5-tr CL (closes top of leaf): (YO [twice], insert hook in next st, YO, draw yarn through st, [YO, draw yarn through 2 lps on hook] twice) 5 times, YO, draw yarn through 6 lps on hook.

SLIP BEAD: On the work, drop the lp from the large hook. Slip one bead on the steel hook. Insert the steel hook in the dropped lp, keeping a firm hold of the lp so that it doesn't enlarge. Apply some tension to the lp to keep it firmly against the tip of the steel hook. Using your right thumb, guide the bead down the hook and onto the lp and draw through only enough lp to accommodate the large hook. Re-insert large hook, continue work, snugging up the next stitch to secure.

INSTRUCTIONS

Capelet is made from the neck down in joined rounds, with RS always facing. BASE CH/SC 88, to measure approx 29" (73cm) stretched, sl st in beg sc to form a ring, being careful not to twist sts. Rnd 1 sets up 8 leaf patt reps of 11 sts.

RND 1: Ch 4, tr2tog in first sc for beg cluster, *ch 5, sk next 4 sc, (SHELL, ch 2, tr) in next sc, (tr, ch 2, SHELL) in next sc, ch 5, sk next 4 sc, CL in next sc; rep from * 7 times, except omit last CL, instead sl st in top of beg cluster: 8 patt reps.

RND 2: (BEG CL, ch 1, CL) in same st, * ch 4, 5-tr CL next shell, ch 5, 3 tr in next tr, 2 tr in next tr, ch 5, 5-tr CL over next 5 tr of shell, ch 4, (CL, ch 1, CL) in next cluster; rep from * 7 times, except omit last cluster, ch 1, and cluster, instead sl st in top of beg cluster.

RND 3: BEG CL, *ch 4, tr in next ch-1 sp, ch 4, CL in next cluster, ch 7, sk next leaf cluster, sc in each of next 5 tr, ch 7, sk next leaf cluster, CL in next cluster; rep from * 7 times, except omit last CL, instead sl st in top of beg cluster.

RND 4: BEG CL, *ch 6, tr in next tr, ch 6, CL in next CL, ch 7, 5-tr CL over next 5 sc, ch 7, CL in next cluster; rep from * 7 times, except omit last CL, instead sl st in beg cluster.

RND 5: BEG CL, *ch 8, (tr, ch 3, tr) in next tr, ch 8, CL in next cluster, ch 6, sc in top of leaf cluster, ch 6, CL in next cluster; rep from *, except omit last CL, instead sl st in beg cluster.

RND 6: BEG CL, *ch 8, SHELL in next tr, ch 2, 2 tr in next ch-3 sp, ch 2, SHELL in next tr, ch 8, CL in next cluster, ch 6, sc in next sc, ch 6, CL in next cluster; rep from * 7 times, except omit last CL, instead sl st in beg cluster.

RND 7: BEG CL, ch 8, sl st in top of beg cluster for picot, *ch 8, 5-tr CL over next shell, ch 5, (SHELL, ch 2, tr) in next tr, (tr, ch 2, SHELL) in next tr, ch 5, 5-tr CL over next shell, ch 8, CL in next cluster, ch 8, sl st in top of last cluster made for picot, CL in next cluster; rep from * 7 times, except omit last picot and CL, instead sl st in top of beg cluster.

RND 8: Sl st to center of first picot, (BEG CL, ch 7, CL) in same sp, *ch 8, sk next leaf cluster, 5-tr CL next shell, ch 7, 3 tr in next tr, 2 tr in next tr, ch 7, 5-tr CL next shell, ch 8, (CL, ch 7, CL) in next picot; rep from * 7 times, except omit last CL, ch 7 and CL, instead sl st in top of beg cluster.

RND 9: BEG CL, *ch 5, CL in next ch-sp, ch 5, CL in next cluster, ch 10, sk next leaf cluster, sc in each of next 5 tr of leaf, ch 10, sk next leaf cluster, CL in next cluster; rep from * 7 times, except omit last CL, instead sl st in beg cluster.

RND 10: BEG CL, *ch 5, (CL, ch 5, CL) in next cluster, ch 5, CL in next cluster, ch 9, 5-tr CL over next 5 sc of leaf, ch 9, CL in next cluster; rep from * 7 times, except omit last CL, instead sl st in beg cluster.

RND 11: BEG CL, *ch 5, CL in next cluster, ch 5, CL in next ch-sp, (ch 5, CL in next cluster) twice, ch 8, sc in top of next leaf cluster, ch 8, CL in next cluster; rep from * 7 times, except omit last CL, instead sl st in beg cluster.

RND 12: BEG CL, *ch 5, CL in next cluster, ch 5, (CL, ch 5, CL) in next cluster, (ch 5, CL in next cluster) twice, ch 8, sc in next sc, ch 8, CL in next cluster; rep from * 7 times, except omit last CL, instead sl st in beg cluster.

Last rnd creates beaded fringe as you go. For fringe without beads, simply omit the instructions: "SLIP BEAD, ch 1" and make the rest the same.

RND 13: BEG CL, *[ch 5, CL in next cluster, make FRINGE by working: ch 5, SLIP BEAD, ch 1, sl st in 5 chs, sl st in top of cluster just made]; rep betw [ ], ch 5, CL in next ch-5 sp, make FRINGE, rep betw [ ] 2 times**; ch 5, CL in next cluster, holding back last 4 lps on hook, CL in next cluster, holding back last 3 lps on hook, YO and draw through all 7 lps on hook, make FRINGE*; rep from * to * 6 times; rep from * ending at **, CL in last cluster, make FRINGE, sl st in top of beg cluster. Fasten off.

finishing

Make band around neck edge.

RND 1 (RS): With RS facing, join yarn with sl st in any base ch of neck, ch 1, sc in same ch, sc in next 87 chs, sl st in beg sc, turn: 88 sc.

RND 2 (WS): Ch 1, (sc in next sc, ch 1, sk next sc) 44 times, sl st in beg sc, turn: 44 ch-sps.

RND 3: Ch 1, (sc in next ch-1 sp, sc in next sc) 44 times, sl st in beg sc. Fasten off.

Weave ends, block capelet to open up stitch pattern and achieve full length.

NOTE: Rnd 2 of neck edge tends to hold in some of the fullness, so neck will measure slightly less than gauge for base ch/sc foundation.

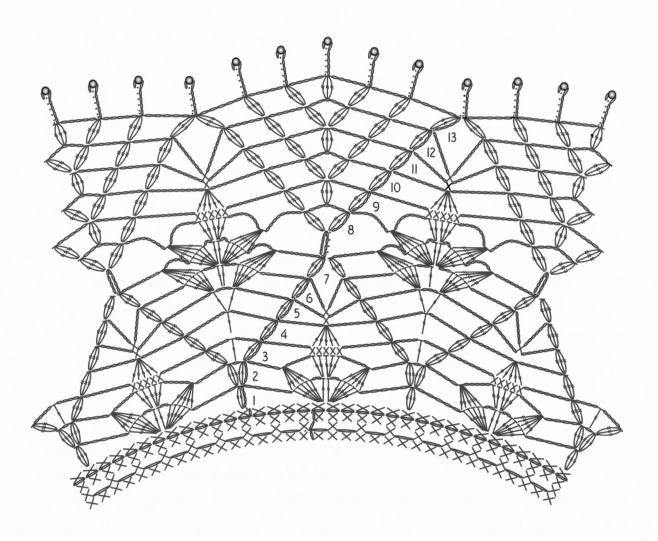

allegheny moon mobius

This mobius, or cowl shape, wraps around your shoulders
and makes soft folds around the neck—a very romantic
look. A basic rectangle is given a half twist and seamed at the
short ends. The yarn is the star of this piece, a fine mohair
blend in a gorgeous colorway, shot with metallic thread.

size

Rectangle: 15" (38cm) wide x 45" (114cm) long before seaming

materials

S. Charles "Ritratto"; 28% mohair, 53% rayon, 10% nylon, 9% polyester; 1¾ oz (50g); 198 yd (180m)

3 balls in #78 (blues)

Size G-7 (4.5mm) crochet hook

Blunt yarn needle

gauge

In patt, one rep = 2" (5cm); 6 rows in patt = 2¼" (6cm)

SPECIAL STITCHES

BASE CH/SC: See Introduction.

TRIPLE CURVE STITCH: Here is the basic stitch pattern. It is a fairly uncomplicated pattern of six rows, easily memorized. The foundation row sets up as many 8-stitch reps as desired onto a BASE CH/SC.

BASE CH/SC a multiple of 8 plus 1 sts.

FOUNDATION ROW: Ch 1, sc in first 3 sts, *ch 5, sk next 3 sts, sc in next 5 sts; rep from * across, except omit last 2 sc, turn.

PATT ROW 1: Ch 1, sc in first 2 sc, *ch 3, sc in next ch-5 sp, ch 3, sk next sc, sc in next 3 sc; rep from * across, except omit last sc, turn.

PATT ROW 2: Ch 1, sc in first sc, *ch 3, sc in next ch-3 sp, sc in next sc, sc in next ch-3 sp, ch 3, sk next sc, sc in next sc; rep from * across, turn.

PATT ROW 3: Ch 5 (counts as dc, ch 2), sc in next ch-3 sp, sc in next 3 sc, sc in next ch-3 sp, *ch 5, sc in next ch-3 sp, sc in next 3 sc, sc in next ch-3 sp; rep from * across to last sc, ch 2, dc in last sc, turn.

PATT ROW 4: Ch 1, sc in first dc, ch 3, sk next sc, sc in next 3 sc, *ch 3, sc in next ch-5 sp, ch 3, sk next sc, sc in next 3 sc; rep from * across to tch sp, ch 3, sc in 3rd ch of tch, turn.

PATT ROW 5: Ch 1, sc in first sc, sc in next ch-3 sp, ch 3, sk next sc, sc in next sc, *ch 3, sc in next ch-3 sp, sc in next sc, sc in next ch-3 sp, ch 3, sk next sc, sc in next sc; rep from * across to last ch-3 sp, ch 3, sc in last ch-3 sp, sc in last sc, turn.

PATT ROW 6: Ch 1, sc in first 2 sc, *sc in next ch-3 sp, ch 5, sc in next ch-3 sp, sc in next 3 sc; rep from *, except omit last sc, turn.

Rectangle is 7 reps wide by 20 reps long.

INSTRUCTIONS

BASE CH/SC 57 to measure 15" (38cm) slightly stretched, set up 7 patt reps.

Work FOUNDATION ROW, then PATT ROWS 1–6 for 19 times, then PATT ROWS 1–5 once more.

NEXT ROW (MAKE CH-3 SPS INSTEAD OF CH-5 SPS): Ch 1, sc in first 2 sc, *sc in next ch-3 sp, ch 3, sc in next ch-3 sp, sc in next 3 sc; rep from * across, except omit last sc, turn.

LAST ROW: Ch 1, sc in first 3 sc, *3 sc in next ch-3 sp, sc in next 5 sc; rep from * across, except omit last 2 sc. Fasten off.

finishing

Weave ends and lightly block rectangle to 15 x 45" (38 x 114cm), opening up the stitch pattern.

Lay rectangle with short ends to each side, long edges at top and bottom. Take two top corners, fold down toward you, overlap the ends and make top corners meet bottom corners. The short ends are now one on top of the other at the bottom. Thread about a yard of yarn on a blunt yarn needle and, matching sts of short ends, whipstitch tog through both thicknesses. Fasten, weave ends.

To wear, hold the seam, keeping it folded at the front, slip the cowl over your head, settle it around your shoulders with the seam going straight across the front, forming a crossover.

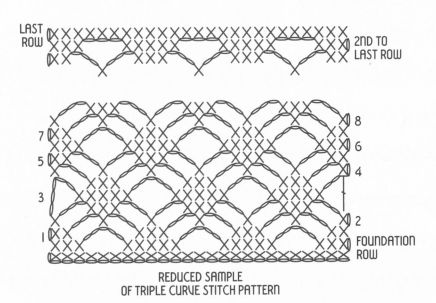

LAST ROW   2ND TO LAST ROW

8
7
6
5
4
3
2
1   FOUNDATION ROW

REDUCED SAMPLE
OF TRIPLE CURVE STITCH PATTERN

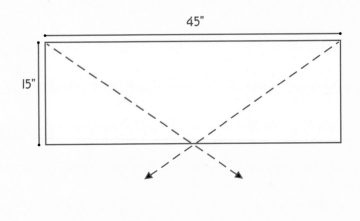

45"

15"

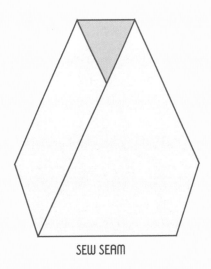

SEW SEAM

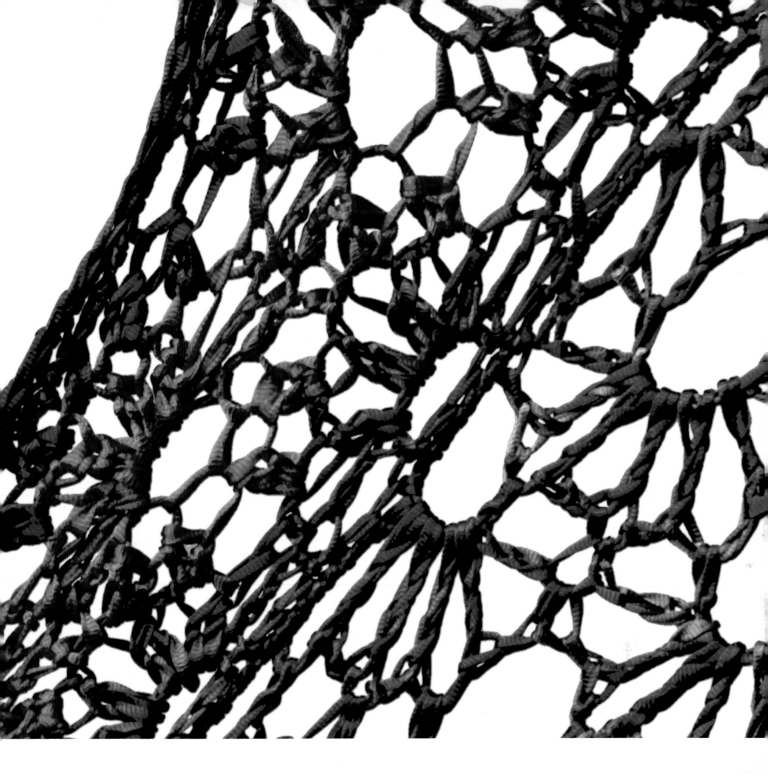

risa robe

This stunning robe, in the sweetest, slinkiest microfiber ribbon yarn, has a way of leaving the private confines of the boudoir and stepping out as eveningwear. It has a retro or ethnic feel to it, part kimono, part Victorian breakfast jacket. Coat length, it features a banded front with contrast floral motif rising to a high back neck, deep V-neck, half-sleeves, and gently scalloped edges with matching sash.

NOTE: The crochet techniques used to make this garment are not difficult, but the yarn is very slippery, gauge is difficult to maintain, and the stitches are harder to see. Therefore, I rate the skill level as experienced.

size

Directions are given for size Small/Medium (S/M). Changes for Large/Extra Large (L/XL) are in parentheses. Sample is size Small/Medium.

Finished bust: 38 (44)" (96.5 (112)cm) excluding band.

Back length from top of band to bottom edge: 29" (74cm).

materials

Tess' Designer Yarns "Microfiber Ribbon"; 100% nylon microfiber; 5 1/4 oz (150g); 333 yd (304m)

3 (4) hanks in Fuchsia (A)

1 hank in Hot Pink (B)

Size I-9 (5.5mm) crochet hook

Split-ring markers or scraps of contrasting yarn for markers

Yarn needle

gauge

12 BASE CH/SC = 4" (10cm) slightly stretched

In FAN patt, one rep (fan, sc) = 2 3/4" (7cm); 4 rows in patt = 3" (7.5cm).

In PETAL STITCH patt of Band or Sash, one rep = 3" (7.5 cm); 9 rows = 2 3/4" (7cm)

NOTE: Resulting fabric is seriously slinky, open and stretchy, nearly impossible to measure, and it will grow and skinny-out when blocked. Keep work loose and relaxed.

SPECIAL STITCHES

BASE CH/SC: See Introduction.

FAN: (Tr, [ch 2, tr] 4 times) in same st or sp.

V-St: (Tr, ch 3, tr) in same st or sp.

CL (cluster)(dc2tog): (YO, insert hook in next st, YO, draw yarn through st, YO, draw yarn through 2 lps on hook) twice in same st or sp, YO, draw yarn through 3 lps on hook.

SCALLOP: (Sl st, ch 3, dc) in same st or sp.

Stitch pattern called "Open Fan" consists of a RS row of fans, and a WS row of ch-sps.

PATT ROW 1: Ch 6 (counts as tr, ch 2), (tr, ch 2, tr) in first ch-sp, *ch 1, sc in next sc, ch 1, sk next dc, FAN in next ch-sp; rep from * across, except omit last FAN, instead work (tr, ch 2) twice in tch sp, tr in 4th ch of tch, turn.

PATT ROW 2: Ch 1, sc in first tr, *ch 3, sk next tr, dc in next ch-sp, ch 2, sk next (tr, sc and tr), dc in next ch-sp, ch 3, sk next tr, sc in next tr; rep from * across, placing last sc in 4th ch of tch, turn.

PATT ROW 3: Ch 1, sc in first sc, *ch 1, sk next dc, FAN in next ch-sp, ch 1, sc in next sc; rep from * across, placing sc in last sc, turn.

PATT ROW 4: Ch 6, sk first sc and next tr, *dc in next ch-sp, ch 3, sk next tr, sc in next tr, ch 3, sk next tr, dc in next ch-sp, ch 2, sk next tr, sc and tr; rep from * across, except after last ch 2, tr in last sc, turn.

INSTRUCTIONS

The robe is made from the neck down, seamlessly. Raglan-type increases in pattern shape the shoulders and at the same time shape the deep V-neck. Sleeves and front band are added later.

NOTE: Mark the center st or sp at each of 4 principal corners and move markers up as you go. Separate instructions for S/M and L/XL follow.

SIZE SMALL/MEDIUM ONLY

With A, BASE CH/SC 33 to measure approx 11" (28cm) slightly stretched.

ROW 1 (RS): Ch 1, sc in first sc, *ch 1, sk next 3 sc, FAN in next sc, ch 1, sk next 3 sc, sc in next sc; rep from * 3 times, ending with sc in last sc, turn: 4 fans.

Set up 4 principal corners and one extra inc at center back.

ROW 2 (INC): Ch 6 (counts as tr, ch 2), V-st in first sc for corner, *ch 2, sk next tr of fan, dc in next ch-2 sp, ch 3, sk next tr, sc in next tr, ch 3, sk next tr, sc in next ch-2 sp, ch 2, V-st in next sc for corner; rep from * 3 times, placing last V-st in last sc, ch 2, tr in same sc, turn: 5 inc corners.

ROW 3: Ch 6, (tr, [ch 2, tr] 3 times) in first ch-sp, *ch 1, sc in ch-sp of next corner V, ch 1, FAN in next ch-sp, ch 1, sc in next sc, ch 1, FAN in next ch-sp; rep from * 4 times, ch 1, sc in ch-sp of next corner V, ch 1, FAN in tch sp, placing last tr of fan in 4th ch of tch, turn: 10 fans.

Discontinue inc at center back, now increase at 4 corners only as follows:

ROW 4 (INC): Ch 6, dc in first ch-sp, *ch 3, sk next tr, sc in next tr, ch 3, sk next tr, dc in next ch-sp, ch 2, V-st in next corner sc, ch 2, sk next tr, dc in next ch-sp, ch 3, sk next tr, sc in next tr, ch 3, sk next tr, dc in next ch-sp**, ch 2, sk next (tr, sc and tr), dc in next ch-sp*; rep from * to * once, (ch 3, sk next tr, sc in next tr, ch 3, sk next tr, dc in next ch-sp, ch 2, sk next [tr, sc and tr], dc in next ch-sp) twice; rep from * to * once; rep from * to ** once, ch 2, tr in 4th ch of tch, turn.

ROW 5: Ch 6, (tr, ch 2, tr) in first ch-sp, *ch 1, sc in next sc, ch 1, sk next dc, FAN in next ch-sp, ch 1, sc in next ch-sp of V, ch 1, FAN in next ch-sp, ch 1, sc in next sc, ch 1, sk next dc, FAN in next ch-sp*; rep from * to * once, (ch 1, sc in next sc, ch 1, sk next dc, FAN in next ch-sp) twice; rep from * to * twice, except omit last fan, instead work (tr, ch 2) twice in tch sp, tr in 4th ch of tch, turn: 13 fans; 2 half fans.

ROW 6 (INC): Ch 1, sc in first tr, ch 3, sk next tr, dc in next ch-sp, ch 2, sk next (tr, sc and tr), dc in next ch-sp, ch 3, sk next tr, sc in next tr, *ch 3, sk next tr, dc in next ch-sp, ch 2, V-st in next corner sc, ch 2, sk next tr, dc in next ch-sp, ch 3, sk next tr, sc in next tr*, (ch 3, sk next tr, dc in next ch-sp, ch 2, sk next [tr, sc and tr], dc in next ch-sp, ch 3, sk next tr, sc in next tr) twice; rep from * to * once, (ch 3, sk next tr, dc in next ch-sp, ch 2, sk next [tr, sc and tr], dc in next ch-sp, ch 3, sk next tr, sc in next tr) 4 times; rep from * to * once, (ch 3, sk next tr, dc in next ch-sp, ch 2, sk next [tr, sc and tr], dc in next ch-sp, ch 3, sk next tr, sc in next tr) twice; rep from * to * once, ch 3, sk next tr, dc in next ch-sp, ch 2, sk next (tr, sc and tr), dc in next ch-sp, ch 3, sk next tr, sc in 4th ch of tch, turn.

ROW 7: Ch 1, sc in first sc, ch 1, sk next dc, FAN in next ch-sp, ch 1, sc in next sc, ch 1, sk next dc, FAN in next ch-sp, *ch 1, sc in next ch-sp of V, ch 1, FAN in next ch-sp*, (ch 1, sc in next sc, ch 1, sk next dc, FAN in next ch-sp) 3 times; rep from * to * once; (ch 1, sc in next sc, ch 1, sk next dc, FAN in next ch-sp) 5 times; rep from * to * once, (ch 1, sc in next sc, ch 1, sk next dc, FAN in next ch-sp) 3 times; rep from * to * once, ch 1, sc in next sc, ch 1, sk next dc, FAN in next ch-sp, ch 1, sc in last sc, turn: 18 fans.

Shape V-neck fronts, work corners even as follows:

ROW 8: Ch 6, sk first sc, ch-sp

and tr, *dc in next ch-sp, ch 3, sk next tr, sc in next tr, sk next tr, dc in next ch-sp, ch 2, sk next (tr, sc and tr); rep from * across, after last ch 2, tr in last sc, turn.

There is a ch-2 sp at each corner.

ROW 9: Ch 6, (tr, [ch 2, tr] 3 times) in first ch-sp, work 17 fans in patt as established, sc in last sc, ch 1, (tr, ch 2) 4 times in tch sp, tr in 4th ch of tch, turn: 19 fans.

There is a fan at each corner.

ROW 10: Ch 6, dc in first ch-sp, *ch 3, sk next tr, sc in next tr, ch 3, sk next tr, dc in next ch-sp, ch 2, sk next (tr, sc and tr), dc in next ch-sp; rep from * across, except omit last dc, after last ch 2, tr in 4th ch of tch, turn.

There is a sc at each corner. Leave markers in these 4 corner sc for sleeves worked later. Join fronts and back with additional sts at underarms as follows:

ROW 11 (JOIN): Ch 6, (tr, ch 2, tr) in first tr, ch 1, sc in next sc, ch 1, *work fans in patt as established to next corner sc, sc in corner sc, ch 1, BASE CH/SC 9, sc in next corner sc, leaving 4 reps of armhole unworked; rep from * once, work 2 fans in patt to end, placing sc in last sc, ch 1, (tr, ch 2) twice in tch sp, tr in 4th ch of tch, turn.

ROW 12: Ch 1, sc in first tr, (ch 3, sk next tr, dc in next ch-sp, ch 2, sk next dc, sc and tr, dc in next ch-sp, ch 3, sk next tr, sc in next tr) twice, *ch 3, sk next tr, dc in next ch-sp, ch 2, sk next (tr, corner sc and first sc of underarm), dc in next sc of underarm, ch 3, sk next 2 sc of underarm, sc in next sc of underarm, ch 3, sk next 2 sc of underarm, dc in next sc, ch 2, sk (last sc of underarm, corner sc and next tr), dc in next ch-sp, ch 3, sk next tr, sc in next tr*; (ch 3, sk next tr, dc in next ch-sp, ch 2, sk next [tr, sc and tr], dc in next ch-sp, ch 3, sk next tr, sc in next tr) 5 times to underarm; rep from * to * once, (ch 3, sk next tr, dc in next ch-sp, ch 2, sk next [tr, sc and tr], dc in next ch-sp, ch 3, sk next tr, sc in next tr) twice, placing last sc in 4th ch of tch, turn.

ROW 13: Ch 1, sc in first sc, *ch 1, sk next dc, FAN in next ch-sp, ch 1, sc in next sc; rep from * across, placing sc in last sc, turn: 13 fans.

Shape V-neck fronts as follows:

ROW 14: Ch 6, sk first sc, ch-sp and tr, *dc in next ch-sp, ch 3, sk next tr, sc in next tr, sk next tr, dc in next ch-sp, ch 2, sk next (tr, sc and tr); rep from * across, after last ch 2, tr in last sc, turn.

ROW 15: Ch 6, (tr, [ch 2, tr] 3 times) in first ch-sp, work 12 fans in patt as established, sc in last sc, ch 1, (tr, ch 2) 4 times in tch sp, tr in 4th ch of tch, turn: 14 fans.

ROW 16: Ch 6, dc in first ch-sp, *ch 3, sk next tr, sc in next tr, ch 3, sk next tr, dc in next ch-sp, ch 2, sk next (tr, sc and tr), dc in next ch-sp; rep from * across, except omit last dc, after last ch 2, tr in 4th ch of tch, turn.

ROWS 17–21: Work PATT ROWS 1–4; then work PATT ROW 1 once more on 14 reps.

Make 2 incs at back as follows:

ROW 22: Ch 1, sc in first tr, *ch 3, sk next tr, dc in next ch-sp, ch 2, sk next (tr, sc and tr), dc in next ch-sp, ch 3, sk next tr, sc in next tr*; rep from * to * 4 times, ch 3, sk next tr, dc in next ch-sp, ch 2, V-st in next sc, ch 2, sk next tr, dc in next ch-sp, ch 3, sk next tr, sc in next tr; rep from * to * twice, ch 3, sk next tr, dc in next ch-sp, ch 2, V-st in next sc, ch 2, sk next tr, dc in next ch-sp, ch 3, sk next tr, sc in next tr; rep from * to * 5 times, placing last sc in 4th ch of tch, turn.

ROW 23: Work as PATT ROW 3, except place sc in ch-sp of each V-st: 16 fans.

ROWS 24–33: Work PATT ROW 4; then work PATT ROWS 1–4 (twice); then work PATT ROW 1 once more: 15 fans; 2 half fans.

Do not turn, continue with A to make Band.

SIZE LARGE/EXTRA LARGE ONLY

ROW 1–7: Same as Size S/M Rows 1–7.

Larger size requires additional

increase rows. This alters the progression of the endings of rows.

Inc at 4 corners and shape V-neck fronts.

ROW 8 (INC): Ch 6, sk first sc, ch-sp and tr, *(dc in next ch-sp, ch 3, sk next tr, sc in next tr, sk next tr, dc in next ch-sp, ch 2, sk next [tr, sc and tr]) to next corner sc, V-st in corner sc, ch 2, sk next tr; rep from * 3 times; (dc in next ch-sp, ch 3, sk next tr, sc in next tr, sk next tr, dc in next ch-sp, ch 2, sk next [tr, sc and tr]) to end, after last ch 2, tr in last sc, turn.

ROW 9: Ch 6, (tr, [ch 2, tr] 3 times) in first ch-sp, work fans in patt as established, placing sc in ch-2 sp of each corner V-st, ending with ch 1, (tr, ch 2) 4 times in tch sp, tr in 4th ch of tch, turn: 23 fans.

ROW 10: Ch 6, dc in first ch-sp, *ch 3, sk next tr, sc in next tr, ch 3, sk next tr, dc in next ch-sp, ch 2, sk next [tr, sc and tr], dc in next ch-sp; rep from * across, except omit last dc, after last ch 2, tr in 4th ch of tch, turn.

There is a ch-sp at each corner.

ROW 11: Work PATT ROW 1.

There is a fan at each corner.

ROW 12: Work PATT ROW 2.

There is a sc at each corner.

Leave markers in these 4 corner sc for sleeves later.

Join fronts and back with additional sts at underarms as follows:

ROW 13 (JOIN): Ch 1, sc in first sc, ch 1, *work fans in patt as established to next corner sc, sc in corner sc, ch 1, BASE CH/SC 9, sc in next corner sc, leaving 5 reps of armhole unworked; rep from * once, work fans in patt to end, placing sc in last sc, turn.

Shape V-neck fronts.

ROW 14: Ch 6, sk first sc, ch-sp and tr, dc in next ch-sp, ch 3, sk next tr, sc in next tr, (ch 3, sk next tr, dc in next ch-sp, ch 2, sk next [tr, sc and tr], dc in next ch-sp, ch 3, sk next tr, sc in next tr) twice, *ch 3, sk next tr, dc in next ch-sp, ch 2, sk next (tr, corner sc and first sc of underarm), dc in next sc of underarm, ch 3, sk next 2 sc of underarm, sc in next sc of underarm, ch 3, sk next 2 sc of underarm, dc in next sc, ch 2, sk (last sc of underarm, corner sc and next tr), dc in next ch-sp, ch 3, sk next tr, sc in next tr*, (ch 3, sk next tr, dc in next ch-sp, ch 2, sk next [tr, sc and tr], dc in next ch-sp, ch 3, sk next tr, sc in next tr) 6 times to underarm; rep from * to * once, (ch 3, sk next tr, dc in next ch-sp, ch 2, sk next [tr, sc and tr], dc in next ch-sp, ch 3, sk next tr, sc in next tr)

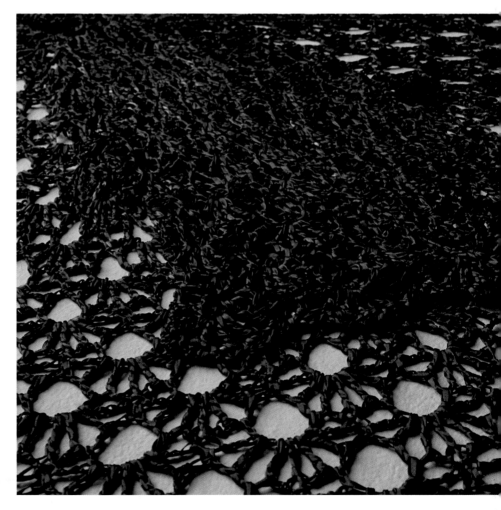

twice, ch 3, sk next tr, dc in next ch-sp, ch 2, tr in last sc, turn.

ROW 15: Ch 6, (tr, [ch 2, tr] 3 times) in first ch-sp, work 14 fans in patt as established, sc in last sc, ch 1, (tr, ch 2) 4 times in tch sp, tr in 4th ch of tch, turn: 16 fans.

ROW 16: Ch 6, dc in first ch-sp, *ch 3, sk next tr, sc in next tr, ch 3, sk next tr, dc in next ch-sp, ch 2, sk next (tr, sc and tr), dc in next ch-sp; rep from * across, except omit last dc, after last ch 2, tr in 4th ch of tch, turn.

ROW 17–23: Work PATT ROWS 1–4; then work PATT ROWS 1–3 once more on 16 reps. Make 2 incs at back as follows:

ROW 24: Ch 6, sk first sc and next tr, *dc in next ch-sp, ch 3, sk next tr, sc in next tr, ch 3, sk next tr, dc in next ch-sp, ch 2, sk next (tr, sc and tr), dc in next ch-sp, ch 3, sk next tr, sc in next tr*; rep from * to * 4 times, ch 3, sk next tr, dc in next ch-sp, ch 2, V-st in next sc, ch 2, sk next tr, dc in next ch-sp, ch 3, sk next tr, sc in next tr; rep from * to * 3 times, ch 3, sk next tr, dc in next ch-sp, ch 2, V-st in next sc, ch 2, sk next tr, dc in next ch-sp, ch 3, sk next tr, sc in next tr; rep from * to * 5 times, ch 3, sk next tr, dc in next ch-sp, ch 2, tr in last sc, turn.

ROW 25: Work as PATT ROW 1, except place sc in ch-sp of each V-st: 18 fans.

ROW 26–33: Work PATT ROW 2–4; then work PATT ROWS 1–4 once; then work PATT ROW 1 once more: 17 fans; 2 half fans.

Do not turn, continue with A to make Band.

BOTH SIZES
band

With RS still facing, rotate and sc evenly along fronts and neck edges as follows.

NOTE: PETAL STITCH patt for Band is worked on a multiple of 9 plus 2 sts, but do not obsess too much over the exact number of sc in Row 1. You can always adjust the pattern sts at either end of Row 2 to compensate.

ROW 1 (RS): Ch 1, 4 sc in each row-end tr, sc in each row-end sc to base ch of neck (93 sc); working across 33 ch sts of neck, sc in next 2 chs, 2 sc in next ch, (sc in next 3 chs, 2 sc in next ch) 7 times, sc in rem 2 ch sts of neck (41 sc); sc across other front edge as before (93 sc), turn: 227 sc. Beg PETAL STITCH patt, 25 9-st reps plus 2.

ROW 2 (FOUNDATION) (WS): Ch 1, sc in first sc, ch 2, sk next sc, *sc in next sc, ch 3, sk next 2 sc, sc in next sc, ch 3, sk next 2 sc, sc in next sc, ch 2, sk next 2 sc; rep from * across, except after last ch 2, sk next sc, sc in last sc, turn.

ROW 3: Ch 3, (CL, ch 2, CL) in first ch-sp, *ch 1, sk next sc and ch-3 sp, sc in next sc, ch 1, sk next ch-3 sp and sc, (CL, [ch 2, CL] 3 times) in next ch-2 sp; rep from * 23 times, ch 1, sk next sc and ch-3 sp, sc in next sc, ch 1, sk next ch-3 sp and sc, (CL, ch 2, CL) in last ch-2 sp, dc in last sc, turn. Fasten off A.

ROW 4: Join B with sl st in first dc, ch 1, sc in same st, *ch 3, CL in top of next 2 clusters, sk next sc, CL in top of next 2 clusters, ch 3, sc in next ch-2 sp; rep from * across, placing last sc in top of tch, turn.

ROW 5: With B, ch 1, sc in first sc, *ch 3, sc in top of next cluster, ch 2, sk next 2 clusters, sc in top of next cluster, ch 3, sc in next sc; rep from * across, turn.

ROW 6: With B, ch 1, sc in first sc, *ch 1, sk next ch-3 sp and sc, (CL, [ch 2, CL] 3 times) in next ch-2 sp, ch 1, sk next sc and ch-3 sp, sc in next sc; rep from * across, turn. Fasten off B.

ROW 7: Join A with sl st in first sc, ch 3, *CL in top of next 2 clusters, ch 3, sc in next ch-2 sp, ch 3, CL in top of next 2 clusters, sk next ch-1 sp, sc and ch-1 sp; rep from * across, except dc in last sc, turn.

ROW 8: With A, ch 1, sc in first dc, ch 2, sk next cluster, *sc in top of next cluster, *ch 3, sc in next sc, ch 3, sc in top of next cluster, ch 2, sk next 2 clusters; rep from * across, except after last ch 2, sc in top of tch, turn.

ROW 9: With A, ch 1, sc in first sc, sc in first ch-2 sp, *sc in next sc, 2 sc in next ch-sp; rep from * across, except make 1 sc in last ch-sp, sc in last sc. Do not turn. With RS still facing, continue with A, rotate and make scallop edging along bottom.

SCALLOP EDGING (RS): Ch 3, dc in first sc row edge of Band, SCALLOP in next row-end dc, sk next row-end sc, SCALLOP in next row-end sc, SCALLOP in next row-end dc, SCALLOP in last row-end sc of Band, SCALLOP in next 2 ch-2 sps of half fan, *SCALLOP in next sc, SCALLOP in next 4 ch-2 sps of fan; rep from * across bottom, except work SCALLOP in 2 ch-sps of last half fan, SCALLOP in first row-end sc of Band, SCALLOP in next row-end dc, sk next sc row edge, SCALLOP in next row-end sc, SCALLOP in next row-end dc, sl st in sc at beg of Band. Fasten off.

sleeves

Worked in joined rnds on 4 (5) skipped reps at armhole, plus one rep across underarm sts. With RS facing, join A with sl st in 5th (middle) ch of underarm.

RND 1 (RS): Ch 6, (tr, ch 2, tr) in same ch, ch 1, sc in next marked corner sc (same as previously worked for join), now working around armhole, *ch 1, sk next dc, FAN in next ch-sp, ch 1, sc in next sc; rep from * 3 (4) times, placing last sc in next marked corner sc

(same as previously worked for join), (tr, ch 2) twice in same ch as beg, sl st in 4th ch of beg ch, turn: 5 (6) fans.

RND 2 (WS): Ch 1, sc in same st, *ch 3, sk next tr, dc in next ch-sp, ch 2, sk next (tr, sc and tr), dc in next ch-sp, ch 3, sk next tr, sc in next tr; rep from * around, except omit last sc, instead sl st in beg sc, turn.

RND 3: Ch 1, sc in same sc, *ch 1, sk next dc, FAN in next ch-sp, ch 1, sc in next sc; rep from * around, except omit last ch 1 and sc, instead sc in beg sc, turn.

RND 4: Sl st in next tr and ch-sp, ch 6 (counts as dc, ch 3), *sk next tr, sc in next tr, ch 3, sk next tr, dc in next ch-sp, ch 2, sk next (tr, sc and tr), dc in next ch-sp, ch 3; rep from * 4 (5) times except omit last (ch 2, tr and ch 3), instead work ch 1, sc in 3rd ch of beg ch, turn.

RND 5: Ch 6, (tr, ch 2, tr) in same sp, *ch 1, sc in next sc, ch 1, sk next dc, FAN in next ch-sp; rep from * around, except omit last fan, instead work (tr, ch 2) twice in same sp as beg, sl st in 4th ch of beg ch, turn.

RNDS 6–11: Rep Rnds 2–5; then rep Rnds 2–3 once more. Do not turn, continue with A to make edging.

SCALLOP EDGING (RS): Ch 3, dc in same sc, *SCALLOP in each of next 4 ch-2 sps of fan, SCAL-LOP in next sc; rep from * around, except omit last SCALLOP, instead sl st in

same sc as beg. Fasten off. Make other sleeve in other armhole in same way. Weave ends and block robe.

sash

NOTE: Sash stretches to approx 60 (66)" (152.5 [167.5]cm) long by 2¾" (7cm) wide when worn.

ROW 1 (RS): With A, BASE CH/SC 163 (179) for 20 (22) 8-st patt reps plus 3. Beg PETAL STITCH patt.

ROW 2 (FOUNDATION) (WS): Ch 1, sc in first sc, ch 2, sk next sc *sc in next sc, ch 3, sk next 2 sc, sc in next sc, ch 3, sk next 2 sc, sc in next sc, ch 2, sk next sc; rep from * across, sc in last sc, turn.

ROW 3–8: Same as ROWS 3–8 of BAND. Fasten off A. Move join to make finishing row that begins by working across one short end.

ROW 9: With RS facing, join A with sl st in ch edge of BASE CH/SC, ch 1, sc in same ch, sc in next row-end "sc" of BASE CH/SC, sc in next row-end sc, 2 sc in next row-end dc, sc in next 3 row-end sc, 2 sc in next row-end dc, 3 sc for corner in last sc, rotate and make sc across long edge as follows: *sc in next ch-2 sp, sc in next sc, 2 sc in next ch-3 sp, sc in next sc, 2 sc in next ch-3 sp, sc in next sc; rep from * to across to last ch-sp, sc in last ch-sp, 3 sc in last sc for corner; rotate and sc across short edge same as other short edge, ending with sc in BASE CH edge. Fasten off. Weave ends.

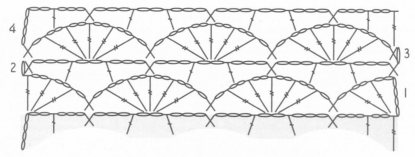

REDUCED SAMPLE OF FAN PATTERN FOR BODY

SCALLOP EDGE

REDUCED SAMPLE OF BAND PETAL PATTERN

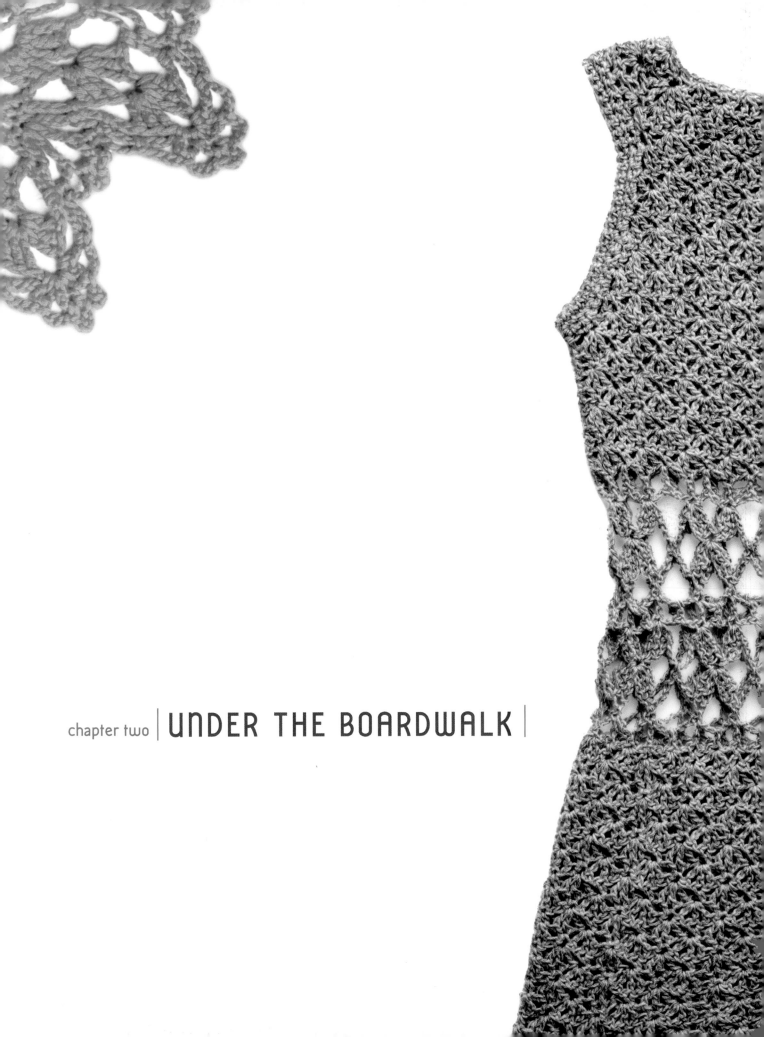

chapter two | UNDER THE BOARDWALK |

heat wave mini-dress

Not for the shy, here's a decidedly retro mini-dress with an open lace midriff, wide-neck tank-style top, and close fit. When you've reached an age at which you no longer willingly display certain parts of your anatomy, simply omit the lace midriff and make the bodice longer to cover what wants covering.

size

Directions are given for size Small (S). Changes for Medium (M) and Large (L) are in parentheses. Sample is size Small.

Finished bust: 35 (38, 42)" (89 [96 1/2, 107]cm)

Back length 29 (29 1/2, 30)" (73.5 [75, 77.5]cm)

NOTE: Dress is very close fitting; however, the fabric is stretchy.

materials

TLC "Cotton Plus"; Art.E516, 51% Cotton, 49% Acrylic; 3 1/2 oz (100g)/178 yd (163m) solid; 3 oz (86g)/155 yd (142m)

4 (5, 6) skeins in #3324 Thistle

Size I-9 (5.5 mm) crochet hook or size needed to obtain gauge

Yarn needle

Split-ring markers or scraps of yarn for markers

gauge

12 BASE CH/SC = 4" (10cm) approx

In SHELL patt, (shell, sc) twice in patt = 3 1/2" (9cm); 8 rows = 4" (10cm)

In CLOVER LEAF LACE patt, one rep = 3 1/2" (9cm); 4 rows = 3 1/2" (9cm)

SPECIAL STITCHES

BASE CH/SC: See Introduction.

SHELL: (Dc, ch 1, dc, ch 1, dc) in same st or sp.

INC SHELL (increase): (Dc, [ch 1, dc] 4 times) in same st or sp.

NOTE: When working in basic SHELL patt, to keep the "seam" (where the rounds are joined and turned) less bulky, use the following method of working the ends of rnds:

RND 2: Ch 1, sc in the next dc, which is the 2nd dc of beg shell, cont in patt around, sl st in beg sc, turn.

RND 3: Ch 3 for 1st dc of beg shell, work around in patt to end, (dc, ch 1, dc) in same sc as beg for 2nd and 3rd dc of beg shell, sc in top of beg ch, turn.

INSTRUCTIONS

Dress is made from the neck down, seamlessly. It has a tank-shaped bodice, with a panel of lace around the midriff, ending in a tiny skirt.

bodice

Begin with a shaped yoke, with corner increases. Divide yoke for front and back, shape armhole edges. Join front and back at under-arm, work until bodice covers bust.

yoke

SIZE SMALL ONLY

BASE CH/SC 56 to measure approx 18" (47 cm) stretched, join with sl st in beg sc to form a ring, being careful not to twist sts.

S RND I (RS): Ch 1, sc in first sc, *sk next sc, SHELL in next sc, sk next sc, sc in next sc; rep from * 13 times, except omit last sc, instead sl st in beg sc, turn: 14 shells.

S RND 2 (WS) (INC RND): Ch 4 (counts as dc, ch 1), (dc, ch 1, dc) in same sc, **sc in 2nd dc of next shell, *SHELL in next sc, sc in 2nd dc of next shell*, INC SHELL in next sc for corner, sc in

2nd dc of next shell, rep from * to * 4 times, INC SHELL for corner in next sc; rep from ** once, except omit last INC SHELL, instead work (dc, ch 1, dc, ch 1) in same sc as beg, sl st in 3rd ch of beg ch to complete corner, turn. To identify corners more easily, place a marker in center of each inc shell (corner), and move markers up as work progresses.

S RND 3 (RS): Ch 3 (counts as dc), sc in next dc, *(SHELL in next sc, sc in 2nd dc of next shell) 5 times, SHELL in 3rd (middle) dc of corner, sc in next dc, (SHELL in next sc, sc in 2nd dc of next shell) twice*, SHELL in 3rd (middle) dc of corner, sc in next dc, rep from * to * once, (dc, ch 1, dc) in same st as beg, sc in top of beg ch, turn: 18 shells.

S RND 4 (WS): Ch 1, sc in next dc, (SHELL in next sc, sc in 2nd dc of next shell) 18 times, except omit last sc, instead sl st in beg sc, turn: 18 shells.

SIZES MEDIUM AND LARGE ONLY

BASE CH/SC 56 to measure approx 18" (47cm) stretched, being careful not to twist sts, join with sl st in beg sc to form a ring.

M/L RND 1 (RS): Ch 1, sc in first sc, *sk next sc, SHELL in next sc, sk next sc, sc in next sc; rep from * 13 times, except omit last sc, instead sl st in beg sc, turn: 14 shells.

M/L RND 2 (WS) (INC RND): Ch 4 (counts as dc, ch 1), (dc, ch 1, dc) in same sc, *sc in 2nd dc of next shell, (SHELL in next sc, sc in 2nd dc of next shell) 4 times, INC SHELL in next sc for corner, sc in 2nd dc of next shell, SHELL in next sc, sc in 2nd dc of next shell, INC SHELL for corner in next sc; rep from * once, except omit last INC SHELL, instead work (dc, ch 1, dc, ch 1) in same sc as beg, sl st in 3rd ch of beg ch to complete corner, turn. To identify corners more easily, place a marker in center of each inc shell (corner), and move markers up as work progresses.

M/L RND 3 (RS) (INC RND): Ch 4 (counts as dc, ch 1), (dc, ch 1, dc) in same st, *sc in next dc, (SHELL in next sc, sc in 2nd dc of next shell) twice, INC SHELL in 3rd (middle) dc of corner, sc in next dc, (SHELL in next sc, sc in 2nd dc of next shell) 5 times, INC SHELL in 3rd dc of corner; rep from * once, except omit last INC SHELL, instead work (dc, ch 1, dc, ch 1) in same dc as beg, sl st in 3rd ch of beg ch to complete corner, turn.

M/L RND 4 (WS): Ch 3 (counts as dc), sc in next dc, *(SHELL in next sc, sc in 2nd dc of next shell) 6 times, SHELL in 3rd (middle) dc of corner, sc in next dc, (SHELL in next sc, sc in 2nd dc of next shell) 3 times*, SHELL in 3rd (middle) dc of corner, sc in next dc; rep from * to * once, (dc, ch 1, dc) in same st as beg, sc in top of beg ch, turn: 22 shells.

M/L RND 5: Ch 1, sc in next dc, (SHELL in next sc, sc in 2nd dc of next shell) 22 times, except omit last sc, instead sl st in beg sc, turn: 22 shells.

ALL SIZES

Divide for front and back, work each side back and forth in rows to underarm.

front

Now work across front body, shape armhole edges.

ROW 1: Ch 4 (counts as dc, ch 1), (dc, ch 1, dc) in same sc for beg shell, (sc in 2nd dc of next shell, SHELL in next sc) 6 (7, 7) times, placing last shell in next corner sc, turn: 7 (8, 8) shells.

SIZE LARGE ONLY

Size Large requires an additional increase row before proceeding.

ROW 1A: Ch 4 (counts as dc, ch 1), (dc, ch 1, dc) in first dc, sc in next dc, (SHELL in next sc, sc in 2nd dc of next shell) 7 times, SHELL in 3rd ch of tch, turn: 9 shells.

ALL SIZES

ROW 2: Ch 4 (counts as dc, ch 1), dc in first dc, sc in next dc, (SHELL in next sc, sc in 2nd dc of next shell) 6 (7, 8) times, (dc, ch 1, dc) in 3rd ch of tch, turn: 6 (7, 8) shells; 2 half shells.

ROW 3: Ch 1, sc in first dc,

(SHELL in next sc, sc in 2nd dc of next shell) 7 (8, 9) times, placing last sc in top of tch, turn.

ROW 4: Ch 4 (counts as dc, ch 1), (dc, ch 1, dc) in first sc, (sc in 2nd dc of next shell, SHELL in next sc) 7 (8, 9) times, turn: 8 (9, 10) shells.

ROWS 5–7: Rep Rows 2–4: 9 (10, 11) shells.

ROW 8: Rep Row 2: 8 (9, 10) shells; 2 half shells. Fasten off.

back

Turn, sk to next corner sc and beg work across Back body. Join with sl st in corner sc, work same as Front. At end of Row 8 do not fasten, instead turn and continue.

Join Front and Back with additional sts at underarm.

JOINING RND: Ch 1, sc in first dc, *(SHELL in next sc, sc in 2nd dc of next shell) 9 (10, 11) times across Back, placing last sc in top of tch of Back, ch 1, BASE CH/SC 5 for underarm*, sc in first dc of front, rep from * to * across front, sl st in beg sc, turn: 20 (22, 24) shells.

body (basic shell pattern)

RND 1: Ch 3 (counts as dc), *sk next 2 sc of underarm, sc in next sc, sk rem 2 sc of underarm, (SHELL in next sc, sc in 2nd dc of next shell) 9 (10,11) times*, SHELL in next sc, rep from * to * once, (dc, ch 1, dc) in same sc as beg, sc in top of beg ch, turn: 20 (22, 24) shells.

RND 2: Ch 1, sc in next dc, (SHELL in next sc, sc in 2nd dc of next shell) 20 (22, 24) times, except omit last sc, instead sl st in beg sc, turn: 20 (22, 24) shells.

RND 3: Ch 3 (counts as dc), sc in 2nd dc of next shell, (SHELL in next sc, sc in 2nd dc of next shell) 19 (21, 23) times, (dc, ch 1, dc) in same sc as beg, sc in top of beg ch, turn: 20 (22, 24) shells.

RND 4–7: Repeat Rnds 2–3 twice.

lace panel
(clover leaf lace pattern)

Worked in joined rnds with RS always facing.

SIZES SMALL AND LARGE ONLY

At end of Rnd 7, turn, sl st in next dc.

SIZE MEDIUM ONLY

Do not turn.

all sizes

RND 8 (RS): Ch 5 (counts as dc, ch 2), (dc in next sc, ch 2, dc in 2nd dc of next shell, ch 2) 19 (21, 23) times, sl st in 3rd ch of beg ch: 40 (44, 48) ch-2 sps.

RND 9: Ch 1, (sc, ch 4, tr2tog) in same st, *sk next dc, (tr2tog, ch 4, sc) in next dc, ch 9, sk next dc, (sc, ch 4, tr2tog) in next dc; rep from * 8 (9, 10) times, sk next dc, (tr2tog, ch 4, sc) in next dc, sk next dc, ch 4, dtr in top of beg sc to complete last ch-sp: 10 (11, 12) patt reps.

RND 10: *Ch 4, sk next tr2tog, (tr2tog, ch 4, sl st, ch 4, tr2tog) in top of next tr2tog, ch 4, sc in next ch-9 sp; rep from * 9 (10, 11) times, except omit last ch 4 and sc, instead tr in top of first dtr at beg of Rnd 9.

RND 11: Ch 1, sc in same tr, (ch 5, sc in top of next tr2tog) 19 (21, 23) times, ch 5, sl st in beg sc: 20 (22, 24) ch-5 sps.

Fasten off.

With RS facing, sk first ch-5 sp, join yarn with sl st in next sc.

RND 12: Ch 5 (counts as dc, ch 2), (dc in next ch-5 sp, ch 2, dc in next sc, ch 2) 19 (21, 23) times, dc in next ch-5 sp, ch 2, sl st in 3rd ch of beg ch: 40 (44, 48) ch-2 sps.

RNDS 13–15: Rep Rnds 9–11. Do not fasten off or move to rejoin yarn. Continue with next rnd.

RND 16: Repeat Rnd 12: 40 (44, 48) ch-2 sps.

skirt

With RS still facing, return to basic SHELL patt as follows:

RND 17 (RS): Ch 1, sc in same st, (SHELL in next dc, sc in next dc) 20 (22, 24) times, except omit last sc, instead sl st in beg sc, turn: 20 (22, 24) shells.

RND 18–37: Rep Body Rnd 3, then Body Rnd's 2–3 9 times, then Body Rnd 2 once more or until dress measures desired length. Fasten off.

Weave ends.

armhole band

Finish armhole edges with a band of sc as follows:

NOTE: To create an armhole that is less likely to gap, make the following rnds of sc firmly. This makes the band lie flat and snug against the body. With RS facing, join yarn in 3rd ch (center) of underarm.

RND 1 (RS): Ch 1, sc in same ch, sc in next 2 ch of underarm, working across armhole edge, sc in each row-end sc, 2 sc in each row-end dc, working across armhole edge of yoke, sc in each dc, ch-1 sp and sc across, sc evenly down other armhole edge same as before, sc in 2 rem ch of underarm, sl st in beg sc, turn.

RND 2 (WS): Ch 1, sc in each sc around, sl st in beg sc, turn.

RND 3 (RS): Rep Rnd 2. Fasten off.

Rep armhole band around other armhole.

Weave ends. Block dress.

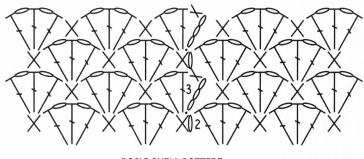

BASIC SHELL PATTERN

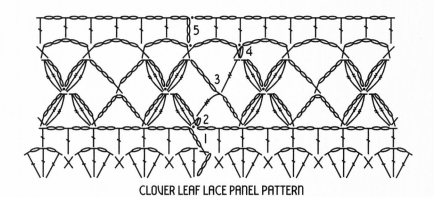

CLOVER LEAF LACE PANEL PATTERN

7   3 (3½, 3½)"

½"

6½ (7, 7½)"

4"

7"

11"

17½ (19, 21)"

shoop-shoop capelet

Top the Heat Wave Mini-Dress with this six-sided capelet that's made like a giant motif with a wedge missing to form the opening. Short and full, it may be worn with open front points or overlapped at the shoulder. When made in a dressy or glitzy yarn, it can also go formal.

size

Directions are given for size Small/Medium (S/M). Changes for Large (L) are in parentheses. Sample is size Small/Medium.

Center back length: 12 (14)" (30.5 [35.5]cm)

Width across bottom edge: 72 (84)" (183 [213]cm)

Width across neck edge: 18" (46cm).

materials

TLC "Cotton Plus"; Art.E516, 51% Cotton, 49% Acrylic; 3½ oz (93g)/178 yd (163m) solid; 3 oz/155 yd (142m)

2 (4) skeins in #3324 Thistle

Size I-9 (5.5mm) crochet hook

Yarn needle

Split-ring markers or scraps of yarn for markers

gauge

12 BASE CH/SC = approx 4" (10cm)

(CL, ch 2) 4 times in patt = 4" (10cm); 4 rows in patt = 4" (10cm).

SPECIAL STITCHES

BASE CH/SC: See Introduction.

tr2tog: (YO [twice], insert hook in ch-sp, YO, draw yarn through ch-sp, [YO, draw yarn through 2 lps on hook] twice) twice in same ch-sp, YO, draw yarn through 4 lps on hook.

tr3tog: (YO [twice], insert hook in ch-sp, YO, draw yarn through ch-sp, [YO, draw yarn through 2 lps on hook] twice) 3 times in same ch-sp, YO, draw yarn through 4 lps on hook.

V-st: (dc, ch 2, dc) in same st or sp.

CL (tr cluster): tr3tog in same st or sp.

INSTRUCTIONS

Pattern stitch is composed of 2 rows, a WS row of dc mesh and a RS row of clusters. Capelet is made from the neck down, with increases at 5 corners, like a giant motif, plus increases at front edges.

NOTE: If you have trouble keeping track of the corners, then go ahead and mark the ch-sp at the center of each V. Move markers up as you go.
BASE CH/SC 37 to measure approx 12" (30.5cm) stretched.

ROW 1 (WS): Ch 5 (counts as dc, ch 2), dc in first sc (counts as first V-st), *(ch 2, sk next sc, dc in next sc) twice, ch 2, sk next sc, V-st in next sc; rep from * 5 times, turn: 25 ch-2 sps.

ROW 2 (RS): Ch 4 (counts as tr), CL in first ch-sp, *(ch 2, CL) in each ch-sp to next V-st, ch 2, (CL, ch 2, CL) in ch-sp of next V-st for corner; rep from * 4 times, (ch 2, CL) in each ch-sp across to end, tr in 3rd ch of tch, turn: 30 CL.

ROW 3: Ch 5 (counts as dc, ch 2), dc in first tr (counts as first V-st), *(ch 2, dc) in each ch-sp across to next corner, ch 2, V-st in corner ch-2 sp; rep from * 5 times, placing last V-st in top of tch, turn: 37 ch-2 sps.

ROWS 4–9: Rep Rows 2–3 (3 times): 66 CL at end of Row 8; 72 ch-2 sps at end of Row 9.

SIZE LARGE ONLY

ROWS 10–11: Rep Rows 2–3: 78 CL at end of row 10; 82 ch-2 sps at end of Row 11.

BOTH SIZES

EDGING: Ch 4, tr2tog in first dc (first half of beg corner), *(ch 2, CL) in each ch-sp across to next V-st, (CL, ch 2, CL) in ch-sp of next V-st; rep from * 4 times, (ch 2, CL) in each ch-sp across to end, (CL, ch 2, CL) in 3rd ch of tch (for corner), ch 2, working across side edge of Capelet, (CL, ch 2) in each row-end st across to neck edge, working across opposite side of BASE CH, sk first ch, (CL in next ch, ch 2, sk next ch) 18 times, working across other side edge, (CL, ch 2) in each row-end st across to bottom edge, CL in same dc as beg to complete first corner, ch 2, sl st in top of beg ch: 118 (134) clusters. Fasten off. Weave ends. Block.

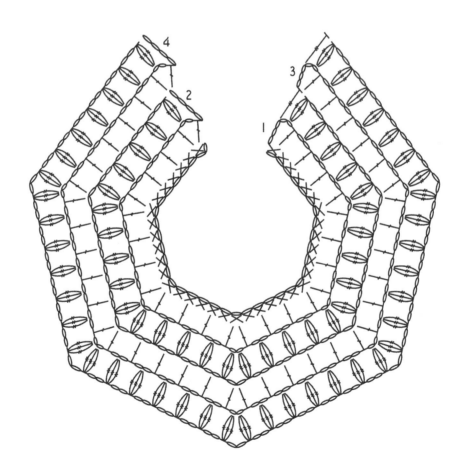

walking after midnight skirt

This flirty skirt, with its cascade of pineapple lace, has terrific movement. It is made from the top down in one piece, fitted to the hip, then flared to the scalloped border that skims the knees. The yarn, a sportweight mercerized cotton, allows this skirt to be comfortably layered over beachwear, jeans, or a slip for dressier occasions.

size

Directions are given for size Small (S). Changes for Medium (M), Large (L), and Extra Large (XL) are in parentheses. Sample is size Small.

Finished waist: 29 (33, 37, 40)" (74 [84, 94, 101.5]cm)

Finished hips: 36 (40, 44, 48)" (91.5 [101.5, 112, 122]cm)

Finished length: 21" (53.5cm) (adjustable)

NOTE: Skirt is close fitting.

materials

Patons "Grace"; 100% mercerized cotton; 1 3/4 oz (50g); 136 yd (125m)

7 (9, 11, 13) balls in #60110 Marine
Size G-7 (4.5mm) crochet hook
Split-ring markers or scraps of contrasting yarn for markers
Yarn needle

gauge

13 BASE CH/SC or sc of waistband = 4" (10cm), slightly stretched

In SHELL patt, 4 shells and 8 rows = 4" (10cm)

In SCALLOP EDGING patt, one rep (fan, sc) = 1 1/2" (4cm)

In DRAWSTRING patt, 8 rows = 4" (10cm)

NOTE: Fabric will grow in length when blocked and worn.

SPECIAL STITCHES

BASE CH/SC: See Introduction.

SHELL: (2 dc, ch 1, 2 dc) in same st or sp.

INC SHELL: (2 dc, ch 1, 2 dc, ch 1, 2 dc) in same st or sp.

FAN: (Tr, [ch 1, tr] 4 times) in same st or sp.

NOTE: When working in basic SHELL patt, to keep the "seam" (where the rounds are joined) less bulky, use this method of working the ends of rnds:

Ch 3, dc in sp for first 2 dc of beg shell, work around in patt to end, 2 dc in same sp as beg for 3rd and 4th dc of beg shell, sc in top of beg ch, turn.

INSTRUCTIONS

Skirt is crocheted from the top down in joined rnds, with RS always facing.

NOTE: Join is located at center back.

BASE CH/SC 96 (108, 120, 132), to measure approx 29 (33, 37, 40)" (74 [84, 94, 101.5]cm) slightly stretched, sl st in beg sc to form a ring, being careful not to twist sts.

RND 1: Ch 3, dc in first sc, sk next 2 sc, (SHELL in next sc, sk next 2 sc) 31 (35, 39, 43) times, sk last 2 sc, 2 dc in same sc as beg, sc in top of beg ch to complete beg shell: 32 (36, 40, 44) shells.

RND 2: Ch 3, dc in first sp, SHELL in ch-sp of next 31 (35, 39, 43) shells, 2 dc in same sp as beg, sc in top of beg ch.

RNDS 3–6: Rep Rnd 2.

Shape hip by inc 4 reps evenly spaced as follows:

RND 7: Ch 3, dc in first sp, SHELL in ch-sp of next 3 (3, 4, 4) shells, *INC SHELL in next ch-sp, SHELL in ch-sp of next 7 (8, 9, 10) shells; rep from * twice, INC SHELL in next ch-sp, SHELL in ch-sp of rem 3 (4, 4, 5) shells, 2 dc in same sp as beg, sc in top of beg ch.

RND 8: Ch 3, dc in first sp, SHELL in next 35 (39, 43, 47) ch-sps, 2 dc in same sp as beg, sc in top of beg ch: 36 (40, 44, 48) shells.

RNDS 9–14: Ch 3, dc in first sp, SHELL in ch-sp of each shell around, 2 dc in same sp as beg, sc in top of beg ch: 36 (40, 44, 48) shells.

NOTE: To alter skirt length, add or omit reps of Rnd 9 here, before further shaping begins.

RND 15: Ch 3, dc in first sp, (ch 1, SHELL in ch-sp of next shell) 35 (39, 43, 47) times, ch 1, 2 dc in same sp as beg, sc in top of beg ch: 36 (40, 44, 48) shells.

RND 16: Ch 3, dc in first sp, (ch 2, SHELL in ch-sp of next shell) 35 (39, 43, 47) times, ch 2, 2 dc in same sp as beg, sc in top of beg ch: 36 (40, 44, 48) shells.

Set up 9 (10, 11, 12) small pineapples as follows:

RND 17: Ch 3, dc in first sp, ch 2, SHELL in ch-sp of next shell, *ch 3, (2 dc, ch 3, 2 dc) in ch-sp of next shell, ch 3, (SHELL in ch-sp of next shell, ch 2) twice, SHELL in ch-sp of next shell; rep from * 8 (9, 10, 11) times, except omit last (SHELL, ch 2 and SHELL), instead work 2 dc in same sp as beg, sc in top of beg ch.

RND 18: Ch 3, dc in first sp, ch 2, SHELL in ch-sp of next shell, *ch 3, sk next ch-3 sp, 7 dc in ch-3 sp of next shell, ch 3, (SHELL in ch-sp of next shell, ch 2) twice, SHELL in ch-sp of next shell; rep from * 8 (9, 10, 11) times, except omit last (SHELL, ch 2 and SHELL), instead work 2 dc in same sp as beg, sc in top of beg ch.

RND 19: Ch 3, dc in first sp, ch 2, SHELL in ch-sp of next shell, *ch 3, dc in next dc, (ch 1, dc in next dc) 6 times, ch 3, (SHELL in ch-sp of next shell, ch 2) twice, SHELL in ch-sp of next shell; rep from * 8 (9, 10, 11) times, except omit last (SHELL, ch 2 and SHELL), instead work 2 dc in same sp as beg, sc in top of beg ch.

RND 20: Ch 3, dc in first sp, ch 3, SHELL in ch-sp of next shell, *ch 3, sc in next ch-1 sp, (ch 3, sc in next ch-1 sp) 5 times, (ch 3, SHELL in ch-sp of next shell) 3 times; rep from * 8 (9, 10, 11) times, except omit last (SHELL, ch 3 and SHELL), instead work 2 dc in same sp as beg, ch 1, sl st in top of beg ch. Fasten off.

Move the join into the next shell, set up 9 (10, 11, 12) big pineapples as follows:

RND 21: With RS facing, join yarn with sl st in ch-sp of next shell, ch 3, dc in first sp, *ch 3, sk next sc, sc in next ch-3 sp, (ch 3, sc in next ch-3 sp) 4 times, ch 3, SHELL in ch-sp of next shell, ch 3 (2 dc, ch 3, 2 dc) in ch-sp of next shell, ch 3, SHELL in ch-sp of next shell; rep from * 8 (9, 10, 11) times, except omit last SHELL, instead work 2 dc in same sp as beg, sc in top of beg ch.

RND 22: Ch 3, dc in first sp, *ch 3, sk next sc, sc in next ch-3 sp, (ch 3, sc in next ch-3 sp) 3 times, ch 3, SHELL in ch-sp of next shell, ch 3, 11 dc in ch-3 sp of next shell, ch 3, SHELL in ch-sp of next shell; rep from * 8 (9, 10, 11) times, except omit last SHELL, instead work 2 dc in same sp as beg, sc in top of beg ch.

RND 23: Ch 3, dc in first sp, *ch 3, sk next sc, sc in next ch-3 sp, (ch 3, sc in next ch-3 sp) twice, ch 3, SHELL in ch-sp of next shell, ch 3, dc in next dc, (ch 1, dc in next dc) 10 times, ch 3, SHELL in ch-sp of next shell; rep from * 8 (9, 10, 11) times, except omit last shell, instead work 2 dc in same sp as beg, sc in top of beg ch.

RND 24: Ch 3, dc in first sp, *ch 3, sk next sc, (sc in next ch-3 sp, ch 3) twice, SHELL in ch-sp of next shell, ch 3, sk next dc, sc in next ch-1 sp, (ch 3, sc in next ch-1 sp) 9 times, ch 3, SHELL in ch-sp of next shell; rep from * 8 (9, 10, 11) times, except omit last shell, instead work 2 dc in same sp as beg, sc in top of beg ch.

RND 25: Ch 3, dc in first sp, *ch 3, sk next sc, sc in next ch-3 sp, ch 3, SHELL in ch-sp of next shell, ch 3, sk next sc, sc in next ch-3 sp, (ch 3, sc in next ch-3 sp) 8 times, ch 3, SHELL in ch-sp of next shell, rep from

* 8 (9, 10, 11) times, except omit last shell, instead work 2 dc in same sp as beg, sc in top of beg ch.

RND 26: Ch 3, dc in first sp, *ch 3, skip next 2 ch-3 sps, SHELL in ch-sp of next shell, ch 3, sk next sc, sc in next ch-3 sp, (ch 3, sc in next ch-3 sp) 7 times, ch 3, SHELL in ch-sp of next shell; rep from * 8 (9, 10, 11) times, except omit last shell, instead work 2 dc in same sp as beg, sc in top of beg ch.

RND 27: Ch 3, dc in first sp, *ch 3, SHELL in next ch-3 sp between shells, ch 3, SHELL in ch-sp of next shell, ch 3, sk next sc, sc in next ch-3 sp, (ch 3, sc in next ch-3 sp) 6 times, ch 3, SHELL in ch-sp of next shell; rep from * 8 (9, 10, 11) times, except omit last shell, instead work 2 dc in same sp as beg, sc in top of beg ch.

RND 28: Ch 3, dc in first sp, *ch 3, INC SHELL in ch-sp of next shell, ch 3, SHELL in ch-sp of next shell, ch 3, sk next sc, sc in next ch-3 sp, (ch 3, sc in next ch-3 sp) 5 times, ch 3, SHELL in ch-sp of next shell; rep from * 8 (9, 10, 11) times, except omit last shell, instead work 2 dc in same sp as beg, sc in top of beg ch.

RND 29: Ch 3, dc in first sp, *ch 3, SHELL in next 2 ch-1 sps of inc shell, ch 3, SHELL in ch-sp of next shell, ch 3, sk next sc, sc in next ch-3 sp, (ch 3, sc in next ch-3 sp) 4 times, ch 3, SHELL in ch-sp of next shell;

rep from * 8 (9, 10, 11) times, except omit last shell, instead work 2 dc in same sp as beg, sc in top of beg ch.

RND 30: Ch 3, dc in first sp, *(ch 3, SHELL in ch-sp of next shell) 3 times, ch 3, sk next sc, sc in next ch-3 sp, (ch 3, sc in next ch-3 sp) 3 times, ch 3, SHELL in ch-sp of next shell; rep from * 8 (9, 10, 11) times, except omit last shell, instead work 2 dc in same sp as beg, sc in top of beg ch.

RND 31: Ch 3, dc in first sp, *ch 3, SHELL in ch-sp of next shell, ch 3, SHELL in next ch-3 sp between shells, (ch 3, SHELL in ch-sp of next shell) twice, ch 3, sk next sc, sc in next ch-3 sp, (ch 3, sc in next ch-3 sp) twice, ch 3, SHELL in ch-sp of next shell; rep from * 8 (9, 10, 11) times, except omit last shell, instead work 2 dc in same sp as beg, sc in top of beg ch.

RND 32: Ch 3, dc in first sp, *ch 3, SHELL in ch-sp of next shell, ch 3, INC SHELL in ch-sp of next shell, (ch 3, SHELL in ch-sp of next shell) twice, ch 3, sk next sc, (sc in next ch-3 sp, ch 3) twice, SHELL in ch-sp of next shell; rep from * 8 (9, 10, 11) times, except omit last shell, instead work 2 dc in same sp as beg, sc in top of beg ch.

RND 33: Ch 3, dc in first sp, *ch 3, SHELL in ch-sp of next shell, ch 3, SHELL in next 2 ch-1 sps of inc shell, (ch 3, SHELL in ch-sp of next shell)

twice, ch 3, sk next sc, sc in next ch-3 sp, ch 3, SHELL in ch-sp of next shell; rep from * 8 (9, 10, 11) times, except omit last shell, instead work 2 dc in same sp as beg, sc in top of beg ch.

RND 34: Ch 3, dc in first sp, (ch 3, SHELL in ch-sp of next shell) 53 (59, 65, 71) times, ch 3, 2 dc in same sp as beg, sc in top of beg ch: 54 (60, 66, 72) shells.

RND 35: Ch 3, dc in first sp, *(ch 3, SHELL) in ch-sp of each of next 5 shells, ch 3, SHELL in next ch-3 sp between shells (over big pineapple), ch 3, SHELL in ch-sp of next shell; rep from * 8 (9, 10, 11) times, except omit last shell, instead work 2 dc in same sp as beg, sc in top of beg ch: 63 (70, 77, 84) shells.

RND 36 (SCALLOP EDGE): Ch 5, (tr, ch 1) 4 times in same sp, *sc in next ch-3 sp, ch 1, FAN in ch-sp of next shell, ch 1; rep from * 61 (68, 75, 82) times, sc in last ch-3 sp, ch 1, sl st in 4th ch of beg ch: 63 (70, 77, 84) fans. Fasten off.

waistband

With RS facing, join yarn with sl st in beg ch of BASE CH.

RND 1: Ch 1, sc in same ch, sc in each ch round, sl st in beg sc: 96 (108, 120, 132) sc.

RND 2: Ch 2, (sk next sc, 2 hdc in next sc) 47 (53, 59, 65) times, sk last sc, hdc in same st as beg, sl st in top of beg ch: 48 (54, 60, 66) sk sc "holes."

RND 3: Sl st in next sp between tch and first hdc (over "hole"), ch 1, 2 sc in same sp, (sk next 2 hdc, 2 sc in next sp between 2 hdc) 47 (53, 59, 65) times, sl st in beg sc. Fasten off.

Weave ends, block skirt.

drawstring

Little back and forth rows make a ¼" (6mm) wide "ribbon" for the Drawstring.

ROW 1: Ch 3, dc in 3rd ch from hook, turn.

ROW 2: Ch 2, dc in first dc, turn.

Rep Row 2 until Drawstring measures approximately 50 (54, 58, 62)" (127 [137, 147.5, 157.5]cm), or your waist measurement plus 24" (61cm). Starting and ending in center front "hole" in Rnd 2 of waistband, weave Drawstring in and out of holes around, pull up ends to gather and tie as desired.

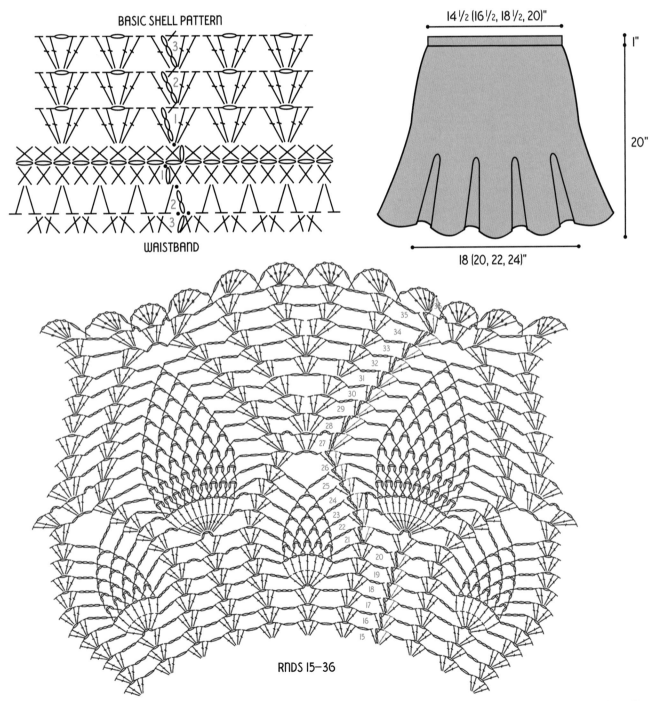

BASIC SHELL PATTERN

WAISTBAND

14 ½ (16 ½, 18 ½, 20)"

1"

20"

18 (20, 22, 24)"

RNDS 15–36

lipstick on your collar

I love the idea of off-the-shoulder tops, but I find them a bit precarious. Here is a compromise. This top has a very wide neckline that hits at the top of the shoulder, still quite bare, but for security has a drawstring and tiny sleeves that hug your upper arms and help the top stay put. The adventurous are welcome to loosen the drawstring and let the top slide all the way off the shoulder. The drawstring serves another purpose. It attaches the lace collar to the neckline by simply threading the string through both thicknesses.

The detachable collar is the crowning glory to this dramatic top. The sample is made in the same yarn, but you can go for greater impact by using any similar weight yarn in a contrasting shade, multicolored or glitzy. Make different collars to suit your mood by adapting your own favorite lace stitch or exploded trim. Simply work enough reps onto the collar foundation (see page 78).

FOR TOP

size

Directions are given for size Extra Small (XS). Changes for Small (S), Medium (M) and Large (L) are in parentheses. Sample is size Extra Small.

Finished bust: 32 (34½, 37, 40)" (81 [87.5 94, 101.5]cm)

Back length from dropped neckline: 16 (16½, 17, 17½)" (40.5 [40.5, 43, 44.5]cm) (hits at top of hip)

materials

South West Trading Company "Oasis"; 100% soy silk; 3½ oz (100g); 240 yd (219m)

2 balls in Perfect Pink

Size H-8 (5mm) crochet hook

Split-ring markers or scraps of contrasting yarn for markers

Yarn needle

gauge

As crocheted:

7 BASE CH/SC = 2" (5cm) slightly stretched

In SHELL patt, one rep (sc, shell) = 1½" (4cm); 6 rows = 2¼" (6cm)

As blocked:

3 reps = 4" (10cm); 6 rows = 2½" (6.5cm)

NOTE: Fabric is extremely soft, loose, and stretchy. Finished top will grow in length and skinny out rather alarmingly.

SPECIAL STITCHES

BASE CH/SC: See Introduction.

SHELL: (Dc, ch 1, dc, ch 1, dc) in same st or sp.

INC SHELL: (Dc, [ch 1, dc] 4 times) in same st or sp.

SCALLOP: (Sl st, ch 2, hdc) in same st or sp.

sctfl: sc working through front loop only of st

NOTE: When working in basic SHELL patt, to keep the "seam" (where the rounds are joined and turned) less bulky, use this method of working the ends of rnds:

RND 2: Ch 3 for first dc of beg shell, work around in patt to end, (dc, ch 1, dc) in same sc as beg for 2nd and 3rd dc of beg shell, sc in top of beg ch, turn.

RND 3: Ch 1, sc in the next dc, which is the 2nd dc of beg shell, cont in patt around, sl st in beg sc, turn.

TOP | INSTRUCTIONS

Top is made from the neck down in one piece in joined rnds, worked back and forth.

Separate instructions for XS, S, M, and L follow.

SIZE EXTRA SMALL ONLY

BASE CH/SC 120 to measure 34" (86.5cm) slightly stretched, sl st in beg sc to form a ring, being careful not to twist sts.

XS RND 1: Ch 1, sc in same sc, (sk next sc, SHELL in next sc, sk next sc, sc in next sc) 30 times, except omit last sc, instead sl st in beg sc, turn: 30 shells.

XS RND 2: Ch 3 (counts as dc), (sc in 2nd dc of next shell, SHELL in next sc) 29 times, sc in 2nd dc of next shell, (dc, ch 1, dc) in same sc as beg, sc in top of beg ch, turn: 30 shells.

XS RND 3: Ch 1, sc in next dc, (SHELL in next sc, sc in 2nd dc of next shell) 29 times, SHELL in next sc, sl st in beg sc, turn: 30 shells.

Make increases at 4 corners as follows.

NOTE: You may wish to mark center st at each corner and move markers up as you go.

XS RND 4 (INC): Ch 4 (counts as dc, ch 1), (dc, ch 1, dc) in same sc for beg corner, *(sc in 2nd dc of next shell, SHELL in next sc) 8 times, sc in 2nd dc of next shell, INC SHELL in next sc, (sc in 2nd dc of next shell, SHELL in next sc) 5 times, sc in 2nd dc of next shell, INC SHELL in next sc; rep from * once more, except omit last INC SHELL, instead (dc, ch 1, dc) in same sc as beg to complete corner, ch 1, sl st in 3rd ch of beg ch, turn: 34 shells.

XS RND 5 (EVEN): Ch 3, sk same ch, sc in next dc, *(SHELL in next sc, sc in 2nd dc of next shell) to next corner, placing last sc in 2nd dc of next corner shell, SHELL in next (center) dc of corner shell, sc in next dc; rep from * 3 times, except omit last shell and sc, instead (dc, ch 1, dc) in same st as beg, sc in top of beg ch, turn: 34 shells.

XS RND 6 (EVEN): Ch 1, sc in next dc, (SHELL in next sc, sc in 2nd dc of next shell) to end, except omit last sc, instead sl st in beg sc, turn: 34 shells.

XS RND 7 (INC): Ch 4, (dc, ch 1, dc) in same sc, *sc in 2nd dc of next shell, (SHELL in next sc, sc in 2nd dc of next shell) to next corner sc, INC SHELL in next corner sc; rep from * 3 times, except omit last inc shell, instead (dc, ch 1, dc) in same st as beg, ch 1, sl st in top of beg ch, turn: 34 shells, 4 of them inc shells.

XS RND 8 (EVEN): Same as XS Rnd 5: 38 shells.

Join front and back with additional sts at underarms as follows:

XS RND 9 (JOIN): Ch 1, sc in next dc, *ch 1, BASE CH/SC 5 for underarm, sk next 7 shells for arm, sc in next corner dc, (SHELL in next sc, sc in 2nd dc of next shell) 11 times, placing last sc in next corner dc; rep from *, except omit last sc, instead sl st in beg sc, turn.

XS RND 10: Ch 3, sc in next dc, *sc in 2nd dc of next shell, (SHELL in next sc, sc in 2nd dc of next shell) 10 times to sc in next corner, SHELL in corner sc, sk next 2 sc of underarm, sc in next sc, sk next 2 sc of underarm, SHELL in next corner sc; rep from *, except omit last shell, instead (dc, ch 1, dc) in same sc as beg, sc in top of beg ch, turn: 24 shells.

SIZE SMALL ONLY

S RND 1: Same as XS Rnd 1: 30 shells.

S RNDS 2–5: Same as XS Rnds 4–7: 34 shells, 4 of them inc shells.

S RNDS 6–8: Same as XS Rnds 5–7: 38 shells, 4 of them inc shells.

S RND 9 (EVEN): Same as XS Rnd 5: 42 shells.

Join front and back with additional sts at underarms as follows:

S RND 10 (JOIN): Ch 1, sc in next dc, * (SHELL in next sc, sc in

2nd dc of next shell) 12 times, placing last sc in next corner dc, ch 1, BASE CH/SC 5 for underarm, sk next 8 shells for arm, sc in next corner dc; rep from *, except omit last sc, instead sl st in beg sc, turn.

S RND 11: Ch 3, sk corner sc, *sk next 2 sc of underarm, sc in next sc, sk next 2 sc of underarm, SHELL in next corner sc, sc in 2nd dc of next shell, (SHELL in next sc, sc in 2nd dc of next shell) 11 times (to sc in next corner), SHELL in corner sc; rep from *, except omit last shell, instead (dc, ch 1, dc) in same sc as beg, sc in top of beg ch, turn: 26 shells.

SIZE MEDIUM ONLY

M RND 1: Same as XS Rnd 1: 30 shells.

M RND 2: Same as XS Rnd 4: 30 shells, 4 of them inc shells.

M RND 3 (INC): Ch 4 (counts as dc, ch 1), (dc, ch 1, dc) in same st (corner dc) for beg corner, *sc in next dc of corner shell, SHELL in next sc, (sc in 2nd dc of next shell, SHELL in next sc) to next corner shell, sc in 2nd dc of corner shell, INC SHELL in next (corner) dc; rep from * 3 times, except omit last INC SHELL, instead (dc, ch 1, dc) in same sc as beg to complete corner, ch 1, sl st in 3rd ch of beg ch, turn: 34 shells, 4 of them inc shells.

M RNDS 4–9: Rep XS Rnds 5–7 (twice): 42 shells, 4 of them inc shells.

M RND 10: Same as XS Rnd 5: 46 shells.

Join front and back with additional sts at underarms.

M RND 11 (JOIN): Ch 1, sc in next dc, *ch 1, BASE CH/SC 5 for underarm, sk next 9 shells for arm, sc in next corner dc, (SHELL in next sc, sc in 2nd dc of next shell) 13 times, placing sc in next corner dc; rep from *, except omit last sc, instead sl st in beg sc, turn.

M RND 12: Ch 3, sc in next dc, *(SHELL in next sc, sc in 2nd dc of next shell) 12 times to sc in next corner, SHELL in corner sc, sk next 2 sc of underarm, sc in next sc, sk next 2 sc of underarm, SHELL in next corner sc, sc in 2nd dc of next shell; rep from *, except omit last shell and sc, instead (dc, ch 1, dc) in same sc as beg, sc in top of beg ch, turn: 28 shells.

SIZE LARGE ONLY

L RND 1: Same as XS Rnd 1: 30 shells.

L RND 2: Same as XS Rnd 4: 30 shells, 4 of them inc shells.

L RND 3: Same as M Rnd 3: 34 shells, 4 of them inc shells.

L RND 4 (INC): Same as M Rnd 3: 38 shells, 4 of them inc shells.

L RNDS 5–10: Rep XS Rnds 5–7 for 2 times: 46 shells, 4 of them inc shells.

L RND 11: Same as XS Rnd 5: 50 shells.

Join front and back with additional sts at underarms.

L RND 12 (JOIN): Ch 1, sc in next dc, * (SHELL in next sc, sc in 2nd dc of next shell) 14 times, placing sc in next corner dc, ch 1, BASE CH/SC 5 for underarm, sk next 10 shells for arm, sc in next corner dc. Rep from *, except omit last sc, instead sl st in beg sc, turn.

L RND 13: Ch 3, sk corner sc, *sk next 2 sc of underarm, sc in next sc, sk next 2 sc of underarm, SHELL in next corner sc, sc in 2nd dc of next shell, (SHELL in next sc, sc in 2nd dc of next shell) 13 times to sc in next corner, SHELL in corner sc. Rep from *, except omit last shell, instead (dc, ch 1, dc) in same sc as beg, sc in top of beg ch, turn: 30 shells.

ALL SIZES
body

Work even on 24 (26, 28, 30) reps for 26 rounds, or to desired length as follows:

RND 1: Ch 1, sc in next dc, (SHELL in next sc, sc in 2nd dc of next shell) 23 (25, 27, 29) times, SHELL in next sc, sl st in beg sc, turn: 24 (26, 28, 30) shells.

RND 2: Ch 3 (counts as dc), (sc in 2nd dc of next shell, SHELL in next sc) 23 (25, 27, 29) times, sc in 2nd dc of next shell, (dc, ch 1, dc) in same sc as beg, sc in top of beg ch, turn: 24 (26, 28, 30) shells.

RNDS 3–26: Rep Rnds 1–2 (12 times) or to desired length. 36 (37, 38, 39) rnds total.

Until now there has been no obvious RS or WS. Turn and make a round of SCALLOP edging on what is now RS.

EDGING (RS): Ch 2, hdc in same sc, *SCALLOP in next sc, SCALLOP in each of next 2 ch-1 sps; rep from * 23 (25, 27, 29) times around lower edge, except omit last scallop, instead sl st in same sc as beg. Fasten off.

Weave ends.

finishing

Make same scallop edging around armholes as follows. With RS facing, locate 3rd (center) base ch at underarm.

ARMHOLE EDGING (RS): Join yarn with sl st in center ch of underarm, ch 2, hdc in same ch, sk next ch, SCALLOP in next ch, *SCALLOP in next ch-1 sp of shell, SCALLOP in next sc, SCALLOP in next ch-1 sp of shell; rep from * 7 (8, 9, 10) times to underarm base ch, SCALLOP in next ch of underarm, sk next ch, sl st in same ch as beg. Fasten off. Work edging around other armhole opening in same way.

NECK EDGING RND 1 (RS): With RS facing, join yarn with sl st in beg base ch of Neck, ch 1, sc in same ch, sc in next 119 ch sts, sl st in beg sc, turn: 120 sc.

RND 2 (WS): Ch 1, (sc in next sc, ch 1, sk next sc) 60 times, sl st in beg sc, turn: 60 ch-sps.

RND 3: Ch 1, (sc in next ch-sp,

sc in next sc) 60 times, sl st in beg sc. Fasten off.

Weave ends, block top to measurements, try not to overly stretch fabric.

drawstring (make 2)

Ch 2, sc in 2nd ch from hook.

ROW 1: Ch 1, without turning, insert hook from top to bottom through front lp of sc just made, sctfl, do not turn.

ROWS 2–100: Ch 1, sctfl of next sc, do not turn.

NOTE: Drawstring should measure approximately 36" (91.5cm) long. Fasten off. Weave ends.

Beg at top center of one shoulder, weave one Drawstring in and out of ch-1 sps of neck band to other shoulder. Weave other Drawstring same way. Tie string ends tog at shoulders and gather neck (or not) as desired.

EDGING

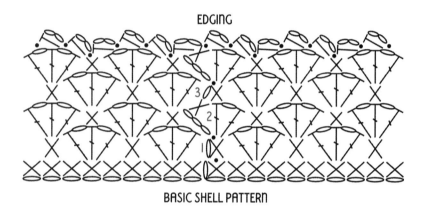

BASIC SHELL PATTERN

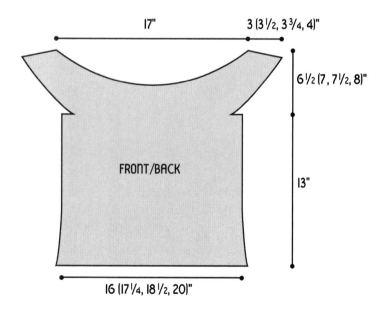

17" 3 (3 1/2, 3 3/4, 4)"

6 1/2 (7, 7 1/2, 8)"

FRONT/BACK

13"

16 (17 1/4, 18 1/2, 20)"

FOR COLLAR

size:

To fit around neckline of top:

Neck edge: 34" (86.5cm) in circumference

Depth: 7" (18cm)

materials

South West Trading Company "Oasis"; 100% soy silk; 3 1/2 oz (100g); 240 yd (219m)

1 ball in Perfect Pink

Size H-8 (5mm) crochet hook

Size G-7 (4.5mm) crochet hook

gauge

With H-8 (5mm) hook, 7 BASE CH/SC = 2" (5cm)

With G-7 (4.5mm) hook, one rep mesh (sc, ch 5) = approx 1" (2.5cm)

SPECIAL STITCHES

BASE CH/SC: See Introduction.

TR SHELL: (3 tr, ch 3, 3 tr) in same st or sp.

V-st (tr, ch 4, tr) in same st or sp.

COLLAR | INSTRUCTIONS

Collar is built onto the same number of neck sts as neck edge of top, worked in joined rnds, with RS always facing.

With H-8 hook, BASE CH/SC 120 to measure 34" (86.5cm) slightly stretched, sl st in beg sc to form a ring, being careful not to twist sts.

RND 1: With G-7 hook, ch 1, sc in same sc, (ch 5, sk next 2 sc, sc in next sc) 39 times, ch 2, dc in beg sc for beg ch-sp: 40 ch-sps.

RND 2: Ch 1, sc in same ch-sp, (ch 6, sc in next ch-sp) 39 times, ch 3, dc in beg sc: 40 ch-sps.

RND 3: Ch 1, sc in same ch-sp, (ch 7, sc in next ch-sp) 39 times, ch 3, tr in beg sc: 40 ch-sps.

RND 4: Ch 4 (counts as tr), 2 tr in same ch-sp, (ch 3, 2 sc in next ch-sp, ch 3, TR SHELL in next ch-sp) 20 times, except omit last tr shell, instead 3 tr in same ch-sp as beg, ch 1, hdc in top of beg ch to complete beg shell: 20 shells.

RND 5: Ch 4, 2 tr in same ch-sp, *ch 4, sc in next ch-sp, sc in next 2 sc, sc in next ch-sp, ch 4, TR SHELL in ch-3 sp of next shell; rep from * 19 times, except omit last tr shell, instead 3 tr in same ch-sp as beg, ch 1, hdc in top of beg ch: 20 shells.

RND 6: Ch 4, 2 tr in same ch-sp, *ch 4, sc in next ch-4 sp, ch 4, sk next sc, sc in next 2 sc, ch 4, sk next sc, sc in next ch-4 sp, ch 4, TR SHELL in ch-3 sp of next shell; rep from * 19 times, except omit last tr shell, instead 3 tr in same ch-sp as beg, ch 1, hdc in top of beg ch: 20 shells.

RND 7: Ch 1, (sc, ch 4, sc) in same sp, *ch 6, hdc in next ch-4 sp, dc in next ch-4 sp, ch 2, V-st between next 2 sc, ch 2, dc in next ch-4 sp, hdc in next ch-4 sp, ch 6**, (sc, [ch 4, sc] 3 times) in ch-3 sp of next tr-shell; rep from * 19 times; rep from * to ** once, (sc, ch 4, sc) in same ch-sp as beg, ch 1, dc in top of beg sc.

RND 8: Ch 1, (sc, ch 4, sc) in same sp, *ch 4, sc in next ch-4 sp, ch 4, sc in next ch-6 sp, ch 4, sk next hdc and dc, sc in next ch-2 sp, ch 4, (sc, ch 4, sc) in ch-4 sp of next V-st, ch 4, sc in next ch-2 sp, ch 4, sk next dc and hdc, sc in next ch-6 sp, ch 4, sc in next ch-4 sp, ch 4, (sc, ch 4, sc) in next ch-4 sp; rep from * 20 times, except omit last (sc, ch 4, sc), instead sl st in beg sc. Fasten off.

neck edging:

With RS facing, with H-8 (5 mm) hook, make edging around neck same as top. Weave ends, block collar. Attach to neckline of top as follows: With RS of both pieces facing, drape collar around outside of top, matching ch-1 sps of neck bands, centering or arranging ruffles of collar as desired. Thread drawstring same way as before, except thread through BOTH thicknesses. Tie strings as desired.

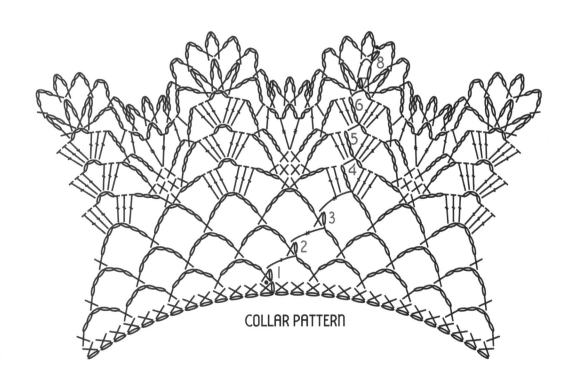

COLLAR PATTERN

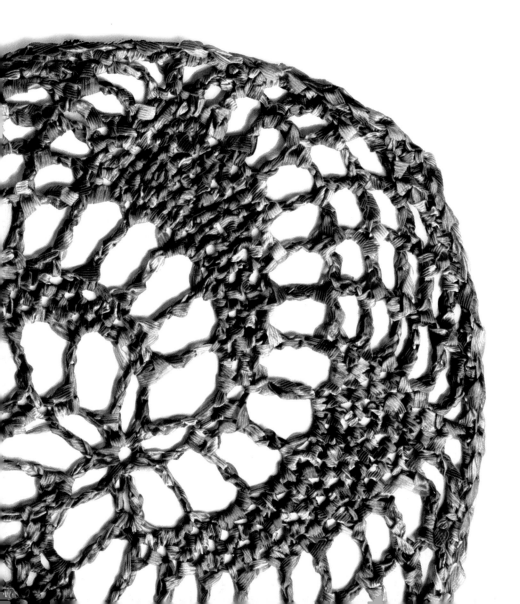

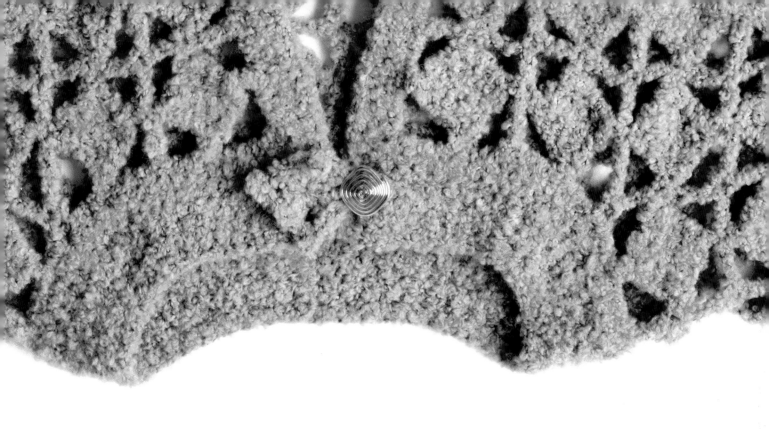

chapter three | SWEET STUFF |

raspberry charlotte poncho and skirt

The top to this fun-to-wear set is a lacy, wrist-length, rounded poncho trimmed with bouncy ball fringe that reminds me of the kitschy lampshades we used to have. The matching skirt is crocheted in a closed half double crochet stitch, with slim fit, a drawstring waist, and above-the-knee length.

size

Lower circumference: approx 60" (152.5cm)

Neck circumference: 24" (61cm)

Length: 19" (48cm) plus bobbles

materials

Berroco "Softwist"; 41% Wool, 59% Rayon; 1¾ oz (50g); 100 yd (92m)

5 hanks in #9420 Nouveau Berry

Size I-9 (5.5mm) crochet hook

Yarn needle

gauge

12 BASE CH/SC = 4" (10cm)

In patt, one rep (fan, sc, ch 5, sc) = 4" (10cm), 4 rows in patt = 2½" (6.5cm)

NOTE: Fabric is enormously stretchy. Measure gauge as crocheted, slightly stretched. This yarn has a bouncy, sort of crunchy hand before blocking, and the poncho will look too short. It will grow considerably when blocked and will also get extremely soft.

SPECIAL STITCHES

BASE CH/SC: See Introduction.

FAN: 7 dc in same sp.

V-st: (Dc, ch 5, dc) in same st.

POPCORN (POP): 7 dc in 4th ch from hook, remove lp from hook, insert hook, from back to front, in top of beg ch (just before the first dc), replace dropped lp on hook and draw through to close pop. The stitches will curl over so the WS of dc will show on the outside of the bobble.

STITCH PATTERN: The stitch pattern is called "Fan Trellis," consisting of a RS row of in-line fans, and a WS row of ch-sps. When making a trellis pattern in the round, I like the following method of joining: The rnds end in the center of the last ch-sp, ready to turn and beg the next rnd; for last ch-5 sp of rnd, ch 2, dc in beg st.

INSTRUCTIONS

Poncho is made from the neck down in joined rnds.

BASE CH/SC 72 to measure approx 24" (61cm) stretched, sl st in beg sc to form a ring, being careful not to twist sts.

Patt begins with 8 reps, but immediately doubles to 16 reps.

RND 1 (WS): Ch 1, sc in same sc, (ch 5, sk next 2 sc, sc in next sc) 24 times, except omit last sc, instead sl st in beg sc, turn: 24 ch-sps.

RND 2 (RS): Ch 8 (counts as dc, ch 5), dc in same sc for beg V-st, *ch 5, sc in next ch-sp, FAN in next ch-sp, sc in next ch-sp, ch 5, V-st in next sc; rep from * 7 times, except omit last ch 5 and V, instead ch 2, dc in 3rd ch of beg ch, turn: 8 fan reps.

RND 3: Ch 1, sc in same sp, *ch 5, sk first dc of fan, sc in next dc, ch 5, sk next 3 dc, sc in next dc, ch 5, sc in next ch-sp, ch 5, (sc, ch 5, sc) in ch-sp of next V-st, ch 5, sc in next ch-sp; rep from * 7 times, except omit last ch 5 and sc, instead ch 2, dc in beg sc, turn.

RND 4: Ch 1, sc in same sp, *FAN in next ch-sp,

sc in next ch-sp, ch 5, sc in next ch-sp; rep from * 15 times, except omit last ch 5 and sc, instead ch 2, dc in beg sc, turn: 16 fan reps.

RND 5: Ch 1, sc in same sp, *ch 5, sk first dc of fan, sc in next dc, ch 5, sk next 3 dc, sc in next dc, ch 5, sc in next ch-sp; rep from * 15 times, except omit last ch 5 and sc, instead ch 2, dc in beg sc, turn.

RNDS 6–25: Repeat Rnds 4–5 for (10 times), or to desired length, ending with Rnd 5 of patt.

RND 26: Ch 3, *FAN in next ch-sp, dc in next ch-sp, ch 7, (POP, sl st) in 4th ch from hook, ch 3, dc in next ch-sp; rep from * 15 times, except omit last dc, instead sl st in top of beg ch. Fasten off.

neck edging

RND 1: With RS facing, join yarn with sl st in any base ch of neck, ch 1, sc in same ch, sc in each ch around, sl st in beg sc, turn: 72 sc.

RND 2: Ch 1, (sc in next sc, ch 1, sk next sc) 36 times, sl st in beg sc, turn: 36 ch-1 sps.

RND 3: Ch 1, (sc in next ch-sp, sc in next sc) 36 times, sl st in beg sc: 72 sc. Fasten off.

finishing

You may make an optional bobble drawstring (see skirt); thread it in and out of the ch-sp holes of Rnd 2.

Weave ends, block poncho, being careful not to stretch it out too much.

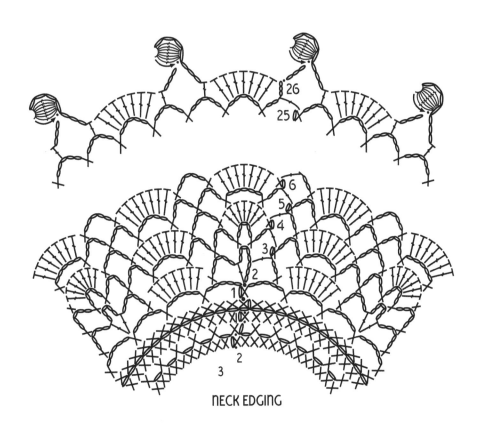

NECK EDGING

FOR SKIRT

size

Directions are given for size Small (S). Changes for Medium (M), Large (L), and Extra Large (XL) are in parentheses. Sample is size Small.

Finished waist: 29 (33, 37, 41)" (74 [84, 94, 104]cm)

Finished hips (measured 8" [20.5cm] below waist): 36 (40, 44, 48)" (91.5 [101.5, 112, 122]cm)

Length: 18" (46cm) plus bobble fringe.

NOTE: Skirt is close fitting.

materials

Berroco "Softwist"; 41% Wool, 59% Rayon; 1¾ oz (50g); 100 yd (92m) 6 (7, 8, 9) hanks in #9420 Nouveau Berry

Size I-9 (5.5mm) crochet hook

Split-ring markers or scraps of yarn for markers

Yarn needle

gauge

12 BASE CH/SC = approx 4" (10cm)

12 hdc and 11 rows hdc = 4" (10cm) (blocks to 10 rows hdc = 4" [10cm])

NOTE: As with poncho, this fabric is enormously stretchy. Measure gauge as crocheted, slightly stretched. This yarn has a bouncy, sort of crunchy hand before blocking, and the skirt will look too short. It will grow considerably in length, skinny out slightly in width, and acquire an extremely soft finish.

Drawstring chain, 14 ch = approx 4" (10cm)

SPECIAL STITCHES

BASE CH/SC: See Introduction.

FAN: 7 dc in same sp.

V-st: (Dc, ch 5, dc) in same st.

POPCORN (POP): 7 dc in 4th ch from hook, remove lp from hook, insert hook, from back to front, in top of beg ch (just before the first dc), replace dropped lp on hook and draw through to close POP. The stitches will curl over so the WS of dc will show on the outside of the bobble.

NOTE: Working hdc in rounds can be tricky. Always ch 2 to begin the round, skip the beg ch, sk the sl st, hdc in next actual hdc.

INSTRUCTIONS

Skirt is crocheted from the waist down in joined rnds of hdc, with shaping at the hip. Bobble trim and waistband are added later.

NOTE: I strongly urge you to use the BASE CH/SC method of foundation. The plain chain foundation will not give you the elasticity needed for this snug, pull-on skirt. If you have any doubts about being able to shimmy into the waistband, then opt to make the next larger size. In any case, work the foundation relaxed, to gauge.

The rnds are joined at the center of left-hand side. To shape the hip, there are increases at four points, like darts. Mark the position of the increase points as well as the st at center of right-hand side, and move markers up as you go.

BASE CH/SC 88 (100, 112, 124) to measure approx 29 (33, 37, 41)" (74 [84, 94, 104]cm), sl st in beg sc to form a ring, being careful not to twist sts.

RND 1 (WS): Ch 2 (counts as hdc), sk first sc, hdc in next 43 (49, 55, 61) sc, hdc and mark in next sc, hdc in each rem 43 (49, 55, 61) sc, sl st in top of beg ch, turn: 88 (100, 112, 124) hdc.

RNDS 2–5: Ch 2, hdc in each hdc around, sl st in top of beg ch, turn: 88 (100, 112, 124) hdc.

RND 6 (INC): Ch 2, *hdc in each of next 11 (13, 15, 17) hdc, 2 hdc in next hdc, hdc and mark in next hdc, hdc in each of next 17 (19, 21, 23) hdc for center panel, hdc and mark in next hdc, 2 hdc in next hdc, hdc in each of next 11 (13, 15, 17) hdc*, hdc and mark in next hdc for right-hand side; rep from * to * once, sl st in top of beg ch, turn: 92 (104, 116, 128) hdc.

NOTE: Maintain the 17 (19, 21, 23) sts of each center panel and the marked sts on either side of the panel constant. Make the increases to the outside of markers.

Now increase 4 sts every other round, moving markers up as you go.

RND 7 (RS) (EVEN): Ch 2, hdc in each hdc, sl st in top of beg ch, turn.

RND 8 (WS) (INC): Ch 2, *hdc in each hdc to st before next marker, 2 hdc in hdc before marker, hdc in marked st and mark, hdc in each of next 17

(19, 21, 23) hdc of center panel, hdc marked st and mark, 2 hdc in next hdc*, hdc in each hdc to side marker, hdc marked side hdc and mark; rep from * to * once, hdc in each hdc to end, sl st in top of beg ch, turn: 96 (108, 120, 132) hdc.

RNDS 9–16: Rep Rnds 7–8 (4 times): 112 (124, 136, 148) hdc at end of last rnd.

RNDS 17–40: Rep Rnd 7 (24 times), or to desired length, ending with a RS rnd. Do not turn. Continue with trim.

bobble trim

Trim requires a multiple of 8 sts. Sizes M, L, and XL need to be adjusted for trim to work out evenly.

NOTE: I like to make trims even, centered at front, back, and sides. Call it obsessive.

SIZE SMALL ONLY

S RND 41 (RS): Sl st in next 2 hdc, ch 1, sc in same hdc, (ch 6, sk next 3 hdc, sc in next hdc) 28 times, except omit last sc, instead sl st in beg sc: 28 ch-sps.

SIZE MEDIUM ONLY

M RND 41 (RS): Sl st in next 2 hdc, ch 1, sc in same hdc, *ch 6, sk next 2 hdc, sc in next hdc, (ch 6, sk next 3 hdc, sc in next hdc) 14 times, ch 6, sk next 2 hdc, sc in next hdc; rep from * once, except omit last sc, instead sl st in beg sc: 32 ch-sps.

SIZE LARGE ONLY

L RND 41 (RS): Sl st in next 2 hdc, ch 1, sc in same hdc, *(ch 6, sk next 2 hdc, sc in next hdc) twice, (ch 6, sk next 3 hdc, sc in next hdc) 14 times, (ch 6, sk next 2 hdc, sc in next hdc) twice; rep from * once, except omit last sc, instead sl st in beg sc: 36 ch-sps.

SIZE EXTRA LARGE ONLY

XL RND 41 (RS): Sl st in next 2 hdc, ch 1, sc in same hdc, *ch 6, sk next 4 hdc, sc in next hdc, (ch 6, sk next 3 hdc, sc in next hdc) 16 times, ch 6, sk next 4 hdc, sc in next hdc; rep from * once, except omit last sc, instead sl st in beg sc: 36 ch-sps.

ALL SIZES

RND 42 (RS): Sl st in next ch-sp, ch 3, 6 dc in same ch-sp, *(dc, ch 7, [POP, sl st] in 4th ch from hook, ch 3, dc) in next ch-sp, FAN in next ch-sp; rep from * 14 (16, 18, 18) times, except omit last fan, instead sl st in top of beg ch. Fasten off.

waistband (3/4" [2cm] wide)

Make Waistband with ch-sp holes for threading drawstring. With RS facing, locate beg st of BASE CH at center of left-hand side.

RND 1 (RS): Join with sl st in beg ch, ch 1, sc in same ch, sc in each of next 87 (99, 111, 123) ch, sl st in beg sc, turn: 88 (100, 112, 124) sc.

RND 2 (WS): Ch 1, sc in same sc, (ch 1, sk next sc, sc in next sc) 44 (50, 56, 62) times, except omit last sc, instead sl st in beg sc, turn: 44 (50, 56, 62) ch-sps.

RND 3: Ch 1, sc in same sc, (sc in next ch-sp, sc in next sc) 44 (50, 56, 62) times, except omit last sc, instead sl st in beg sc: 88 (100, 112, 124) sc. Fasten off.

Weave ends and block skirt before threading Drawstring.

drawstring

Drawstring has a popcorn at each end, which is too bulky for threading, so you will make one popcorn attached to the string, thread the string, then complete the popcorn at the other end.

Ch 150 (160, 170, 180), or make a ch, to gauge, that equals the skirt waistband measurement plus 12" (30.5cm), (POP, sl st) in 4th ch from hook, sl st in each ch to end. Fasten off temporarily, leaving a 1 yd (0.9m) tail to complete POP after weaving. Beginning at center front, thread tail in and out of ch-sps of waistband, draw a few inches of Drawstring through last ch-sp. Pick up lp from temporary fastening, ch 3, (POP, sl st) in 4th ch from hook. Fasten off. Weave ends.

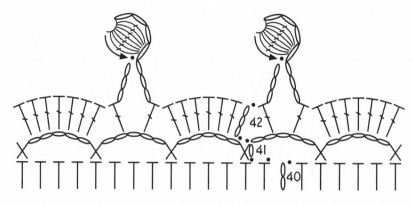

BUBBLE TRIM FOR SKIRT

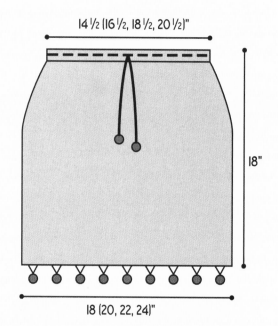

14 1/2 (16 1/2, 18 1/2, 20 1/2)"

18"

18 (20, 22, 24)"

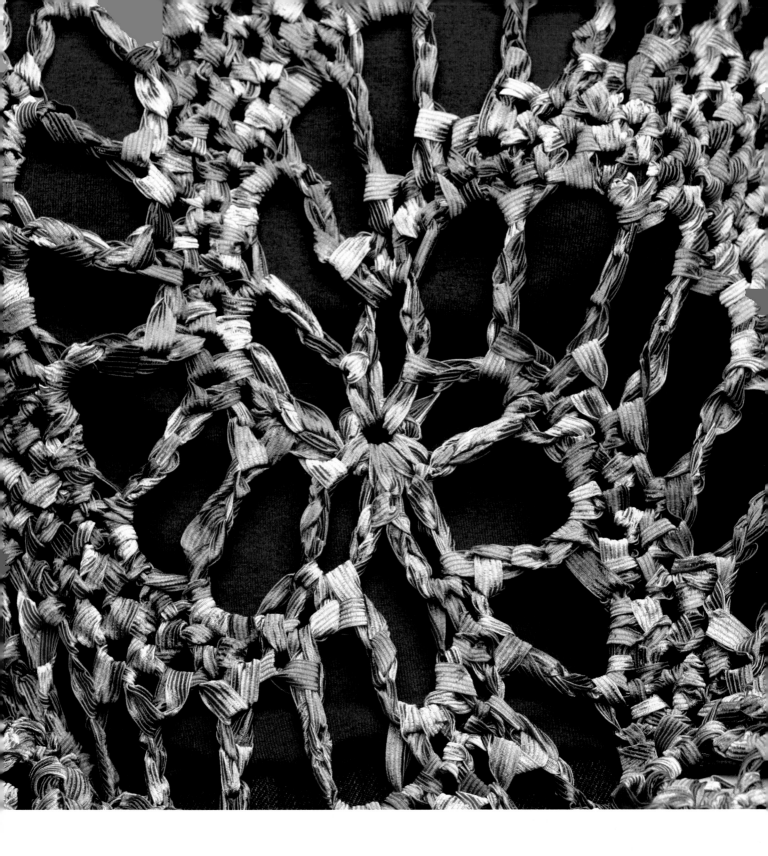

farpoint topper

Here is a motif I've always wanted to use in a garment, but until this design I could never figure out how to do it. Four identical spiral pentagrams are joined into a cone shape that's flattened, then seamed for sleeves. Wonder of wonders, this topper looks great on everyone who has tried it on. It's roomy and comfortable, and it stretches to fit most figures to XL.

size

One size fits most

Finished bust: 44" (112cm)

Back length: 20" (51cm)

Sleeve length: 13" (33cm)

materials

Lion Brand "Incredible"; Art #520; 100% nylon ribbon; 1³/₄ oz (50g); 110 yd (100m)

6 balls in #206 Autumn Leaves

Size N-13 (9mm) crochet hook

Split-ring marker or scrap of contrasting yarn for marker

Large, blunt yarn needle for assembly (I prefer ball-end for this job)

gauge

8 sc = 4" (10cm)

Motif measures 13" (33cm) along each side, 20" (51cm) in diameter across widest point (before assembly)

Keep work relaxed

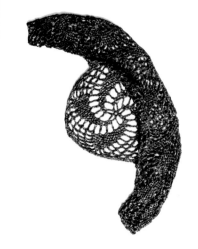

INSTRUCTIONS

Make 4 pentagram Motifs. Join according to diagram.

motif (make 4)

Made in continuous rounds with RS always facing.

NOTE: Mark last sc of each rnd and move marker up to next rnd as work progresses.

Ch 5, sl st in 5th ch from hook to form a ring.

RND 1: (Ch 6, sc) 5 times in ring, mark last sc: 5 ch-sps.

RND 2: (Ch 6, 3 sc in next ch-6 sp) 5 times: 5 sections of 3 sc.

RND 3: (Ch 6, 3 sc in next ch-6 sp, sc in next 2 sc of section, sk last sc of section) 5 times: 5 sections of 5 sc.

RND 4: (Ch 6, 3 sc in next ch-6 sp, sc in next 4 sc of section, sk last sc of section) 5 times: 5 sections of 7 sc.

RND 5: (Ch 6, 3 sc in next ch-6 sp, sc in next 6 sc of section, sk last sc of section) 5 times: 5 sections of 9 sc.

RND 6: (Ch 6, 3 sc in next ch-6 sp, sc in next 8 sc of section, sk last sc of section) 5 times: 5 sections of 11 sc.

RND 7: (Ch 6, 3 sc in next ch-6 sp, sc in next 10 sc of section, sk last sc of section) 5 times: 5 sections of 13 sc.

RND 8: *Ch 5, sc in next ch-6 sp, ch 5, sk first sc of section, sc in next 11 sc, sk last sc of section; rep from * 4 times: 5 sections of 11 sc.

RND 9: *(Ch 5, sc in next ch-5 sp) twice, ch 5, sk first sc of section, sc in next 9 sc, sk last sc of section; rep from * 4 times: 5 sections of 9 sc.

RND 10: *(Ch 5, sc in next ch-5 sp) 3 times, ch 5, sk first sc of section, sc in next 7 sc, sk last sc of section; rep from * 4 times: 5 sections of 7 sc.

RND 11: *(Ch 5, sc in next ch-5 sp) 4 times, ch 5, sk first sc of section, sc in next 5 sc, sk last sc of section; rep from * 4 times: 5 sections of 5 sc.

RND 12: *(Ch 5, sc in next ch-5 sp) 5 times, ch 5, sk first sc of section, sc in next 3 sc, sk last sc of section; rep from * 4 times: 5 sections of 3 sc.

RND 13: Ch 5, sc in next ch-5 sp, *(ch 3, sc in next ch-5 sp) 5 times, ch 3, sk first sc of section, dc in next sc, sk last sc of section, ch 3, sc in next ch-5 sp; rep from * 4 times, except omit last sc, instead sl st in beg sc: 35 ch-3 sps.

RND 14: Ch 1, **sc in sc, *2 sc in next ch-3 sp, sc in next sc*; rep from * to * once, 5 sc in next ch-3 sp for corner, sc in next sc, rep from * to * twice, 2 sc in next ch-3 sp, sc in next dc, 2 sc in next ch-3 sp: rep from ** 4 times, sl st in beg sc: 1 sc in each corner; 23 sc across each side between corners. Fasten off.

Weave ends. Block Motifs all to same dimensions.

assembly

With RS facing, arrange Motifs following construction diagram.

Each Motif has 5 sides and 5 corners. One Motif is the front, one is the back, and there is one for each sleeve. One of the 5 sides of front and back Motifs is the neckline. One of the 5 corners of each sleeve is positioned at neck.

Beginning at underarm, sew up one armhole to neck, down other side of armhole to underarm, and sew sleeve seam as follows:

Thread a long length of yarn onto a large, blunt-end yarn needle. Hold tog right sleeve Motif with front Motif, matching the middle sc of corner at underarm, 23 sc, middle sc of corner at neck. Join yarn in corner sc through both thicknesses, whipst tog through both thicknesses to next corner sc. Hold back Motif in place, whipst tog neck corner sc through three thicknesses. Drop front Motif. Hold back Motif tog with sleeve, matching 23 sc, whipst through both thicknesses to next underarm corner sc. Fold sleeve Motif in half, bringing corresponding corners tog, whipst through three thicknesses at underarm corner sc. Drop back Motif. Hold sleeve edges tog, matching 23 sc, whipst tog through both thicknesses, whipst tog last corner sc. Fasten off.

Attach other sleeve same way. Weave ends.

finishing

NOTE: I find the neck opening too stretchy and loose. If you need a more secure neck, feel free to make the finishing round of sl st tight, or use a smaller hook, to hold in some of the fullness. If the opening is okay as is, then sl st to gauge.

NECK EDGE: With RS facing, join with sl st in corner sc of neck, firmly sl st in each sc around neck edge, sl st in beg sc. Fasten off.

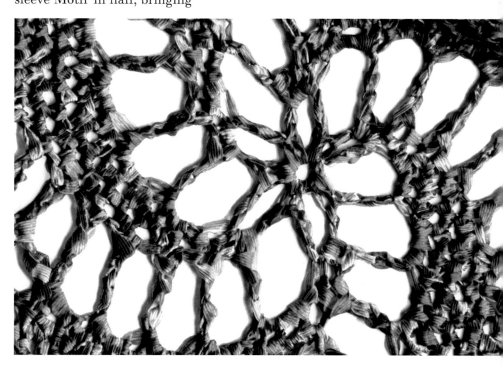

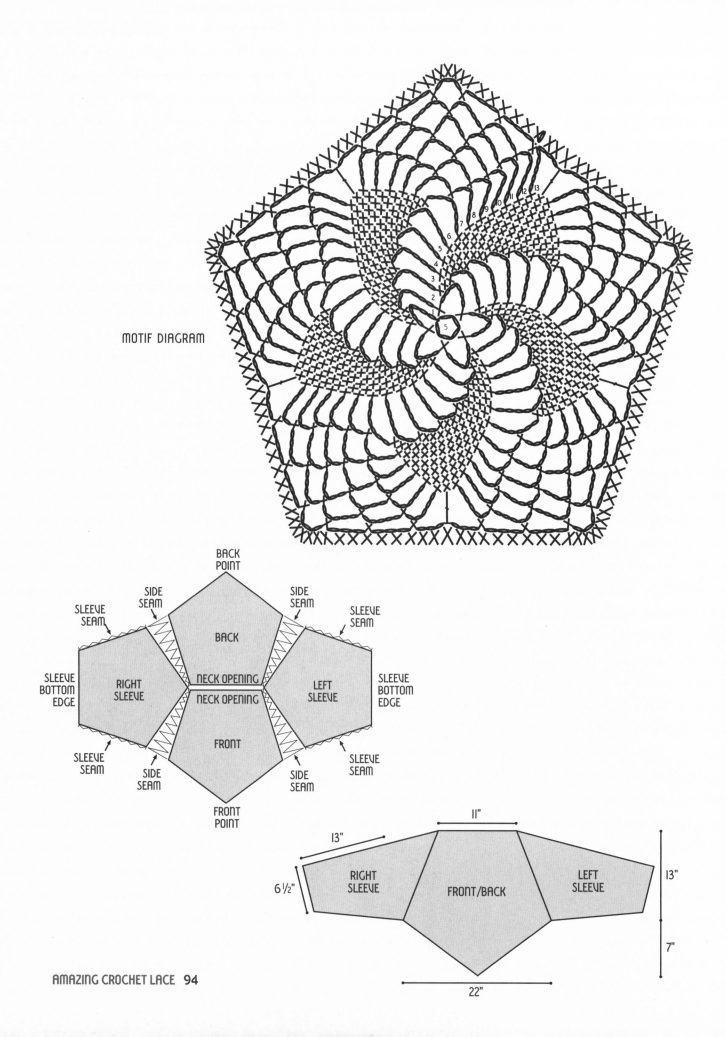

MOTIF DIAGRAM

BACK
POINT

SIDE
SEAM

SIDE
SEAM

SLEEVE
SEAM

SLEEVE
SEAM

BACK

SLEEVE
BOTTOM
EDGE

RIGHT
SLEEVE

NECK OPENING

LEFT
SLEEVE

SLEEVE
BOTTOM
EDGE

NECK OPENING

SLEEVE
SEAM

FRONT

SLEEVE
SEAM

SIDE
SEAM

SIDE
SEAM

FRONT
POINT

11"

13"

RIGHT
SLEEVE

FRONT/BACK

LEFT
SLEEVE

13"

6 1/2"

7"

22"

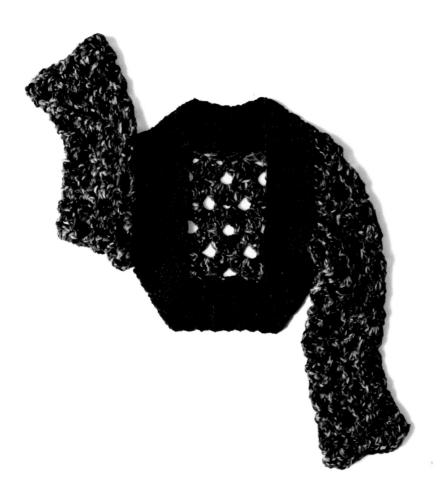

rocky road shrug

Deep, rich autumn shades are used for this shrug. The interesting, abbreviated shape is just a jacket with no fronts, featuring long, slightly flared sleeves. A chunky yarn and big hook make the body quick to crochet. The wide band of ribbing in a luscious suede yarn keeps the piece snug against the neck and across the upper back.

size

Directions are given for size Small/Medium (S/M). Changes for Large/Extra Large (L/XL) are in parentheses. Sample is size Small/Medium.

Back width, at underarm above ribbing: 15 (18)" (38 [46]cm).

Back length, including ribbing: 15 (16½)" (38 [42]cm).

materials

Lion Brand "Landscapes"; 50% wool, 50% acrylic; 1¾ oz (50g); 55 yd (50m)

4 (5) balls in #282 River Crossing (A)

Lion Brand "Lion Suede"; 100% polyester; 3 oz (85g); 122 yd (110m)

1 (2) skeins in #126 Coffee (B)

Size M-13 (9mm) crochet hook

Size K-10½ (6.5mm) crochet hook, for ribbing

Split-ring markers or scraps of contrasting yarn for markers

Large, blunt yarn needle

gauge

With A, using M-13 (9mm) hook, 7 BASE CH/SC = approx 4" (10cm)

In patt, one rep (sc, ch 1, shell, ch 1) = 3" (7.5cm); 4 rows = 3½" (9cm).

With B, using K-10½ (6.5mm) hook, in ribbing, 9 sts of band = 3" (7.5cm); 6 rows = 3" (7.5cm).

INSTRUCTIONS

Body of shrug is crocheted from the neck down in one piece. The sleeves and ribbed band are worked on later.

body

With A and larger hook, BASE CH/SC 13 to measure 7½" (19cm) slightly stretched.

ROW 1 (RS): Ch 4 (counts as dc, ch 1), (dc, ch 1, dc, ch 1, dc) in first sc, *ch 1, sk next sc, sc in next sc, ch 1, sk next sc, SHELL in next sc; rep from * twice, placing last shell in last sc, turn: 4 shells.

ROW 2 (WS) (INC): Ch 5 (counts as dc, ch 2), *sc in first ch-sp of shell, ch 3, sk next ch-sp of shell, sc in next ch-sp of shell, ch 3, V-st in next sc, ch 3, sk first dc of next shell*, sc in first ch-sp of shell, ch 3, sk next ch-sp of shell, sc in next ch-sp of shell, sk first dc of next shell; rep from * to * once, sc in first ch-sp of shell, ch 3, sk next ch-sp of shell, sc in next ch-sp of shell, ch 2, dc in 3rd ch of tch, turn.

ROW 3: Ch 4, (dc, ch 1, dc, ch 1, dc) in next ch-sp, (ch 1, sc in next ch-sp, ch 1, SHELL in next ch-sp) 6 times, placing last shell in tch sp, last dc in 3rd ch of tch, turn: 7 shells.

ROW 4 (INC): Ch 5 (counts as dc, ch 2), *sc in first ch-sp of shell, ch 3, sk next ch-sp of shell, sc in next ch-sp of shell, ch 3, sk first dc of next shell, sc in first ch-sp of shell, ch 3, sk next ch-sp of shell, sc in next ch-sp of shell, ch 3, V-st in next sc, ch 3, sk first dc of next shell, sc in first ch-sp of shell, ch 3, sk next ch-sp of shell, sc in next ch-sp of shell, ch 3, sk first dc of next shell; rep from * once, sc in first ch-sp of shell, ch 3, sk next ch-sp of shell, sc in next ch-sp of shell, ch 2, dc in 3rd ch of tch, turn.

ROW 5: Ch 4, (dc, ch 1, dc, ch 1, dc) in next ch-sp, (ch 1, sc in next ch-sp, ch 1, SHELL in next ch-sp) 9 times, placing last shell in tch sp, last dc in 3rd ch of tch, turn: 10 shells.

SIZE SMALL/MEDIUM ONLY

ROW 6: Ch 5 (counts as dc, ch 2), *sc in first ch-sp of shell, ch 3, sk next ch-sp of shell, sc in next ch-sp of shell, ch 3, sk first dc of next shell; rep from * 9 times, except omit last ch 3, instead work ch 2, dc in 3rd ch of tch, turn.

ROW 7: Ch 3, (dc, ch 1, dc) in first ch-sp, (ch 1, sc in next ch-sp, ch 1, SHELL in next ch-sp) 9 times, ch 1, sc in next ch-sp, ch 1, (dc, ch 1, dc) in tch sp, dc in 3rd ch of tch, turn: 9 shells; 2 half shells.

ROW 8: Ch 4 (counts as hdc, ch 2), *sk next ch-sp of shell, sc in next ch-sp of shell, sk first dc of next shell, sc in first ch-sp of shell, ch 3; rep from * 9 times, except omit last ch 3, instead work ch 2, hdc in top of tch, turn.

ROW 9: Ch 1, sc in first hdc, ch 1, sk ch-2 sp, (SHELL in next ch-sp, ch 1, sc in next ch-sp, ch 1) 10 times, except omit last ch 1, place last sc in 2nd ch of tch, turn: 10 shells.

ROW 10 (INC): Ch 5 (counts as dc, ch 2), *(sc in first ch-sp of shell, ch 3, sk next ch-sp of shell, sc in next ch-sp of shell, ch 3, sk first dc of next shell) twice, sc in first ch-sp of shell, ch 3, sk next ch-sp of shell, sc in next ch-sp of shell, ch 3, V-st in next sc, ch 3, sk first dc of next shell, sc in first ch-sp of shell, ch 3, sk next ch-sp of shell, sc in next ch-sp of shell, ch 3, sk first dc of next shell; rep from * once, (sc in first ch-sp of shell, ch 3, sk next ch-sp of shell, sc in next ch-sp of shell, ch 3, sk first dc of next shell) twice, except omit last ch 3, instead work ch 2, dc in 3rd ch of tch. Fasten off.

SIZE LARGE/ EXTRA LARGE ONLY

ROW 6 (INC): Work same as S/M Row 10.

ROWS 7–11 (EVEN): Work same as S/M Rows 5–9: 13 shells.

ROW 12: Ch 5 (counts as dc, ch 2), *(sc in first ch-sp of shell, ch 3, sk next ch-sp of shell, sc in next ch-sp of shell, ch 3, sk first dc of next shell) 3 times, sc in first ch-sp of shell, ch 3, sk next ch-sp of shell, sc in next ch-sp of shell, ch 3, V-st in next sc, ch 3, sk first dc of next shell*, (sc in first ch-sp of shell, ch 3, sk next ch-sp of shell, sc in next ch-sp of shell, ch 3, sk first dc of next shell) 4 times, sc in first ch-sp of shell, ch 3, sk next ch-sp of shell, sc in next ch-sp of shell, ch 3; rep from * to * once, (sc in first ch-sp of shell, ch 3, sk next ch-sp of shell, sc in next ch-sp of shell, ch 3, sk first dc of next shell) 3 times, except omit last ch 3, instead work ch 2, dc in 3rd ch of tch. Fasten off.

left sleeve

NOTE: Mark ch-sp of 2 V-st at back corners, leave markers for joining band.

With RS facing, bring left front point to meet V-st at left back, work across armhole and join, work sleeve in joined rounds as follows:

RND 1: With RS facing, using M-13 hook, join A in ch-3 sp of V-st at left back corner, ch 1, sc in same sp, ch 1, working across left front, (SHELL in next ch-sp, ch 1, sc in next ch-sp, ch 1) 3 (4) times around armhole, SHELL in last ch-sp, sc in beg sc, turn: 4 (5) shells.

RND 2: Sl st in next dc and ch-sp of shell, ch 1, sc in same ch-sp, (ch 3, sk next ch-sp of shell, sc in next ch-sp, ch 3, sk first dc of next shell, sc in next ch-sp) 3 (4) times, ch 3, sk next ch-sp of shell, sc in next ch-sp, ch 1, dc in beg sc, turn.

RND 3: Ch 4, (dc, ch 1, dc) in same sp, (ch 1, sc in next ch-sp, ch 1, SHELL in next ch-sp) 3 (4) times, ch 1, sc in next ch-sp, ch 1, dc in same ch-sp as beg, sc in 3rd ch of beg ch, turn.

RND 4: Ch 1, sc in same sp, (ch 3, sk first dc of next shell, sc in next ch-sp, ch 3, sk next ch-sp, sc in next ch-sp) 3 (4) times, ch 3, sk first dc of next shell, sc in next ch-sp, ch 1, dc in beg sc, turn.

RND 5: Ch 1, sc in same sp, (ch 1, SHELL in next ch-sp, ch 1, sc in next ch-sp) 3 (4) times, ch 1, SHELL in next ch-sp, sc in beg sc, turn.

RNDS 6–19: Rep Rows 2–5 (3 times); then rep Rows 2–3 once more. Fasten off.

right sleeve

RND 1: With RS facing, using M-13 hook, join A with sl st in ch-3 sp of V-st at right back corner, ch 1, sc in same sp, working toward front point, (SHELL in next ch-sp, ch 1, sc in next ch-sp) 3 (4) times around armhole, SHELL in last ch-sp at front point, bring to meet back corner, sc in beg sc, turn: 4 (5) shells.

RNDS 2–19: Rep Rnds 2–19 of Left Sleeve. Weave ends.

band

NOTE: Worked in a slightly smaller gauge, the first rnd of sc will hold in some of the fullness, particularly across the back.

Go to marker at V-st at right underarm, with RS facing, make a rnd of sc evenly around entire edge as follows:

EDGING (RS): With K-10½ (6.5mm) hook, join B with sl st in marked ch-sp, ch 1, sc in same sp, sc in each row-end sc, sc in each row-end hdc, 2 sc in each row-end dc along shap-

ing at right front, sc in 13 ch sts of neck, sc along left front same as before to marked ch-sp of V-st at left underarm, sc in marked sp, sc in next dc of V-st (sc in each ch of next ch-3 sp, sc in next sc) 9 (11) times, placing last sc in next dc of V-st at beg, sl st in beg sc: 97 (113) sc. **NOTE:** The exact number of sc is not critical!

ribbing

NOTE: Ribbing is crocheted firmly, to make a snug band.

ROW 1: Ch 1, sc in same sc, insert hook in 2 forward strands of stem of sc just made, BASE CH/SC 8, turn: 9 sc.

ROW 2 (WS): Ch 1, sc in first sc, sctbl in next 8 sc, sl st in next 2 sc of edge, turn.

ROW 3: Sk sl st, sctbl in next 8 sc, sc both lps of last sc, turn. Rep Rows 2–3 around entire edging. Fasten off, leaving a long sewing length.

Hold last row tog with base ch, with RS of edges facing each other, matching sts, whipst tog through both thicknesses. Fasten off. Weave ends.

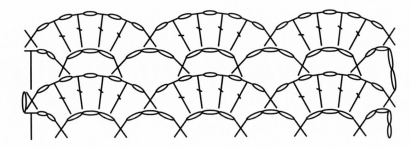

REDUCED SAMPLE OF
BASIC SHELL PATTERN

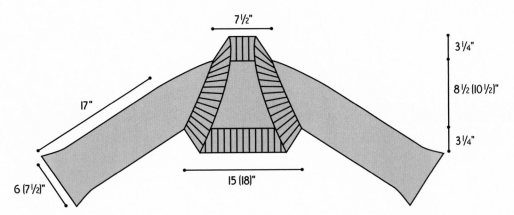

pumpkin pie jacket

This jacket is made seamlessly from the bottom up—not my usual MO, but in this case it's the best way to attack the bold pattern of boxes. This jacket is a "rib tickler," with elbow-length sleeves, banded edges, a wide rounded collar, and front closure options. The yarn is a bulky-weight bouclé with a touch of stretch and subtle shading that is quite lovely.

NOTE: Sizing is achieved by adjusting the gauge. Unfortunately, there are no standard hooks available in sizes between the K-10½ (6.5mm) and the L-11 (8mm). In order to make the Medium size, you will need to choose one or the other and adjust your tension, so some experience is required for this project.

size

Directions are given for size Small (S). Changes for Medium (M) and Large (L) are in parentheses. Sample is size Small.

Finished bust: 36 (40, 44)" (91.5 [101.5, 112]cm)

Back length: 13 (14½, 16)" (33 [37, 40.5]cm)

NOTE: Garment is close fitting.

materials

Lily Chin Signature Collection "Central Park"; 37% wool, 39% acrylic, 15% polyester, 7% viscose, 2% Lycra; 1¾ oz (50g); 96 yd (88m)

5 (6, 7) balls in #3776 (rust)

Size G-7 (4.5mm) crochet hook for button loop (optional)

Size K-10½ (6.5mm) crochet hook, for size S

Size L-11 (8mm) crochet hook, for size L

NOTE: For size M, use either size K-10½ (6.5mm) or size L-11 (8mm), whichever achieves required gauge.

Purchased button, or set of frogs or clasps, as desired

Yarn needle

gauge

For size S, using K-10½ (6.5mm) hook, 11 BASE CH/SC = 4" (10cm), 2 patt reps (12 sts) and 4 rows = 4½" (11.5cm) square

For size M, using K-10½ (6.5mm) hook loosely, or L-11 (8mm) hook tightly, 10 BASE CH/SC = 4" (10cm), 2 reps and 4 rows = 5" (13cm) square

For size L, using L-11 (8mm) hook, 9 BASE CH/SC = 4" (10cm), 2 reps and 4 rows = 5½" (14cm) square

NOTE: Due to the texture and the added Lycra in the yarn, this fabric does not change much when blocked. Crocheted measurements accurately reflect the finished measurements.

SPECIAL **STITCHES**

BASE CH/SC: See Introduction.

Stitch pattern consists of a RS row of diamond-shaped boxes, and a WS row of ch-sps that completes the frame around each box.

BOX: Ch 1, sc in first sc, 3 sc in next ch-3 sp, (turn, ch 1, sc in next 4 sc) 3 times.

INSTRUCTIONS

Jacket is made from the bottom up in one piece.

NOTE: The same instructions apply for all sizes. Use whatever hook size and tension you need to achieve the correct gauge for your size.

body

BASE CH/SC 97 to measure approx 36 (40, 44)" (91.5 [101.5, 112]cm) slightly stretched.

ROW 1 (RS): Ch 6 (counts as dc, ch 3), sk first sc, sk next 2 sc, sc in next sc, turn, work BOX, sk next 2 sc of base ch, dc in next sc, ch 3, sk next 2 sc of base ch, sc in next sc; rep from * 15 times, except omit last ch 3 and sc, end with dc in last sc of base ch, turn: 16 boxes.

ROW 2 (WS): Ch 6 (counts as tr, ch 2), *sc in sc at top corner of next box, ch 2, tr in next dc, ch 2; rep from * 15 times, except omit last ch 2, end with tr in 3rd ch of tch, turn.

ROW 3: Ch 6, *sc in next sc, turn, work BOX, dc in next tr, ch 3; rep from * 15 times, except omit last ch 3, place last dc in 4th ch of tch, turn.

ROW 4: Rep Row 2.

Divide and separately work 4 reps for each front, 8 reps for back as follows:

right front

ROW 1: Ch 6, *sc in next sc, turn, work BOX, dc in next tr, ch 3; rep from * 3 times, except omit last ch 3, turn, leaving remaining sts unworked: 4 boxes.

ROW 2 (WS): Ch 6, *sc in sc at top corner of next box, ch 2, tr in next dc, ch 2; rep from * 3 times, except omit last ch 2, end with tr in 3rd ch of tch, turn.

ROW 3: Ch 6, *sc in next sc, turn, work BOX, dc in next tr, ch 3; rep from * 3 times, except omit last ch 3, place last dc in 4th ch of tch, turn.

ROW 4: Rep Row 2. Fasten off.

Shape front neck as follows:

ROW 5 (RS): Sk first 2 tr (2 box reps), join yarn with sl st in next tr, ch 6, work in pattern as Row 3 for 2 reps: 2 boxes.

ROW 6: Rep Row 2.

ROW 7: Rep Row 3. Fasten off.

left front

With RS facing, sk next 8 box reps of body, join yarn with sl st in next tr.

ROW 1: Ch 6, *sc in next sc, turn, work BOX, dc in next tr, ch 3; rep from * 3 times, except omit last ch 3, place last dc in 4th ch of tch, turn: 4 boxes.

ROWS 2–4: Work even in established pattern.

Shape front neck as follows:

ROW 5: Ch 6, *sc in next sc, turn, work BOX, dc in next tr, ch 3; rep from * once more, except omit last ch 3, turn, leaving remaining sts unworked: 2 boxes.

ROW 6–7: Work even in established pattern. Fasten off.

back

With RS facing, locate same tr in Row 4 of Body where last st of right front Row 1 is worked.

ROW 1: Join yarn with sl st in same tr, ch 6, *sc in next sc, turn, work BOX, dc in next tr, ch 3; rep from * 7 times, except omit last ch 3, working last dc in same tr as first st of left front Row 1, turn: 8 boxes.

ROWS 2–5: Work even in established pattern.

Join back to left front at shoulder, continue in patt across back, then join back to right front shoulder as follows:

JOINING ROW: Hold first 2 boxes of back tog with 2 boxes of left front to join left shoulder, ch 4, tr in first dc of left front, *ch 2, sc in sc at top of next box of back, sc in sc at top of next box of left front, ch 2, tr in next dc of back, tr in next dc of left front; rep from * once; working across back only, **ch 2, sc in sc at top corner of next box, ch 2, tr in next dc; rep from ** 3 times; hold last 2 boxes of back tog with 2 boxes of right front to join right shoulder, tr in first dc of right front; rep from * twice across right front. Fasten off.

first sleeve

With RS facing, locate tr at center of underarm previously joined for front and back.

RND 1 (RS): Join yarn with sl st in same tr, ch 6, working along armhole edge, *sc in row edge above next box, turn, work BOX, dc in row edge above next "frame line," ch 3; rep from * 5 times, sc in row edge above last box, turn, work BOX, sl st in 3rd ch of beg ch, turn: 7 boxes.

RND 2 (WS): Ch 6, *sc in sc at top corner of next box, ch 2, tr in next dc, ch 2; rep from * 6 times, except omit last tr and ch 2, instead sl st in 4th ch of beg ch, turn.

RND 3: Ch 6, *sc in next sc, turn, work BOX, dc in next tr, ch 3; rep from * 6 times, except omit last dc and ch 3, instead sl st in 3rd ch of beg ch, turn.

RNDS 4–6: Rep Rnds 2–3; then rep Rnd 2 once more.

Make band as follows:

RND 7 (RS): Ch 1, sc in same st, *2 sc in next ch-2 sp, sc in next sc, 2 sc in next ch-2 sp, sc in next tr; rep from * 6 times, except omit last sc, instead sl st in beg sc, turn: 42 sc.

RND 8: Ch 1, sc in each sc around, sl st in beg sc, turn.

RND 9: Ch 1, sc in each sc around, sl st in beg sc. Fasten off.

Rep sleeve in other armhole in same way.

finishing

Make band around edge of jacket, add collar, complete finishing edge as follows:

With RS facing, locate BASE CH/SC row edge at lower corner of right front.

RND 1 (RS) (FRONT AND NECK ONLY): Join with sl st in row-end sc, ch 1, sc in same st, 3 sc in each ch-sp along Right Front, 9 sc in upper corner ch-sp (31 sc); 3 sc in each ch-sp around front neck shaping, Back neck and Left Front neck shaping (66 sc); 9 sc in upper corner ch-sp, 3 sc in each ch-sp along Left Front, sc in row-end sc of BASE CH/SC at lower corner (31 sc), turn: 128 sc.

RND 2 (WS) (ENTIRE JACKET): Ch 1, sc in each sc around fronts and neck, working 3 sc in center (5th) sc of upper corners. At lower right front, make 3 sc in last sc, rotate, sc in each base ch of lower edge, 2 sc in same sc as beg, sl st in bag sc: 233 sc. Fasten off.

collar

Worked onto 78 sc of neck.

With RS facing, locate center (2nd) sc at upper corner of right front.

Dec 6 sc evenly spaced across as follows:

ROW 1 (RS) (DEC): Join with sl st in corner sc, ch 1, sc in same sc, sc in next 7 sc, (sc2tog, sc in next 10 sc) 5 times, sc2tog in next 2 sts, sc in next 8 sc, turn: 72 sc.

ROW 2 (DEC): Ch 1, sc in first sc, sc in next 7 sc, (sc2tog, sc in next 9 sc) 5 times, sc2tog in next 2 sts, sc in last 7 sc, turn: 66 sc.

ROW 3 (DEC): Ch 1, sc in first sc, sc in next 6 sc, (sc2tog, sc in next 8 sc) 5 times, sc2tog in next 2 sts, sc in last 7 sc, turn: 60 sc.

ROW 4 (DEC): Ch 1, sc in 1st sc, sc in next 6 sc, (sc2tog, sc in next 7 sc) 5 times, sc2tog in next 2 sts, sc in last 6 sc, turn: 54 sc.

EDGING: Ch 1, sc in first sc, sc in next 52 sc of collar, 3 sc in last sc, rotate, sc in each of next 4 row-end sc of collar, sc in each sc around jacket edge, working 3 sc in center of lower corners, at other side of collar, sc in each of next 4 row-end sc, 2 sc in same sc as beg. Fasten off. Weave ends. Block or lightly steam jacket, gently flattening out boxes and bands, giving collar a rounded shape.

button loop
(approx 2½" [6.5cm] tip to tip) (optional)

Here's a chance to show off that single button (orphaned, but really special) you've collected. The sample shows the loop with a purchased button.

motif

With G-7 hook, leaving a long tail, ch 4, sl st in beg ch to form a ring.

RND 1: Ch 3, dc in ring, *ch 4, sl st in 3rd ch from hook for picot, ch 1, 3 dc in ring; rep from * twice, ch 6 for button loop, dc in ring, sl st in 3rd of beg ch. Fasten off. Weave in ending tail. Use beg tail to secure motif to right front corner of collar. Sew button to left front corner of collar opposite button loop.

If you prefer, sew your choice of clasp or frog closure to fronts.

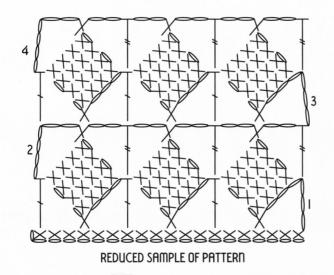

REDUCED SAMPLE OF PATTERN

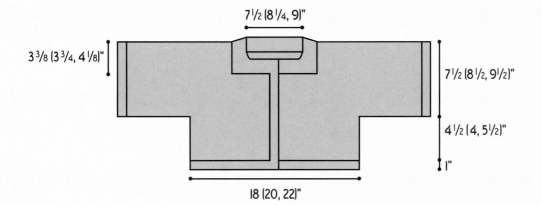

7½ (8¼, 9)"

3⅜ (3¾, 4⅛)"

7½ (8½, 9½)"

4½ (4, 5½)"

1"

18 (20, 22)"

pistachio parfait ruana

A ruana (pronounced "roo-WAN-na") is a South American, particularly Colombian, outer garment, usually woven of heavy wool. It is a square or rectangle, with a slit from the center of the neck to the bottom that divides the front into two pieces, while the back remains solid.

To crochet a ruana, you only need to start at the bottom of the back, work to the neck, then work each half of the front separately. This yarn makes a velvety-soft wrap that can go from casual to dressy in a heartbeat.

size

Rectangle with two rectangles attached

Back width: 47" (119.5cm)

Back length: 24" (61cm)

Front width: 22" (56cm) each

Front length: approximately 27" (68.5cm)

materials

TLC "Amore"; Art.E515; 80% acrylic, 20% nylon; 6 oz (171g); 290 yd (266m) solid; 4½ oz (128g)/223 yd (204m)

5 skeins in Amazon #3260

Size I-9 (5.5mm) crochet hook

gauge

In patt, one rep and 6 rows = 2½" (6.5cm). (This fabric is stretchy, and the weight of the ruana will make it grow in length.)

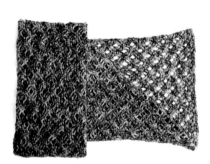

SPECIAL STITCH

TRIPLE CURVE STITCH: Refer to Allegheny Moon Mobius (page 42).

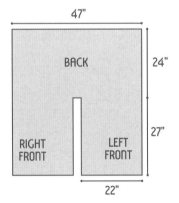

INSTRUCTIONS

Back is 17 reps wide by 10 reps long; divide for fronts with one rep unworked at center back neck. Fronts are 8 reps wide by 11 reps long.

back

BASE CH/SC 137, to measure approx 47"

(119.5cm) slightly stretched, set up 17 patt reps. Work FOUNDATION ROW, then PATT ROWS 1–6 for 9 times, then PATT ROWS 1–5 once more.

front

Divide for neck and fronts as follows:

NEXT ROW (SAME AS PATT ROW 6): Ch 1, sc in first 2 sc, *sc in next ch-3 sp, ch 5, sc in next ch-3 sp, sc in next 3 sc; rep from * 7 more times, except omit last sc, turn, leaving rem sts unworked: 8 patt reps for front.

Now working across 8 reps of one front, rep PATT ROWS 1–6 for 10 times, PATT ROWS 1–5 once more.

NEXT ROW (MAKE CH-3 SPS INSTEAD OF CH-5 SPS): Ch 1, sc in first 2 sc, *sc in next ch-3 sp, ch 3, sc in next ch-3 sp, sc in next 3 sc; rep from * across, except omit last sc, turn.

LAST ROW: Ch 1, sc in first 3 sc, *3 sc in next ch-3 sp, sc in next 5 sc; rep from * across, except omit last 2 sc. Fasten off.

Return to neck, leave sc at center of neck unworked, join with sl st in next ch-3 sp, ch 1, work same way as other front.

Weave ends.

chapter four | LAST CALL |

sambuca jacket

Black lace is universally considered sexy. Here is an alluring cardigan jacket, crocheted in a fan pattern in black merino wool. It is cropped to a slightly fitted waist, with a jewel neckline and long sleeves, and is closed at the neck with a purchased sweater clasp. Due to the stretchiness of the lace, this cardigan has a roomy, forgiving fit.

size

Directions are given for size Small/Medium (S/M). Changes for sizes Large (L) and Extra Large (XL) are in parentheses. Sample shown in size Small/Medium.

NOTE: Size XL will fit up to 48" (122cm) bust.

Finished bust: 38 (44, 50)" (96.5 [112, 127]cm)

Back length: 16 (17, 18)" (40.5 [43, 46]cm)

Sleeve length: 17 (18, 17)" (43 [46, 43]cm)

materials

Filatura di Crosa "Zara"; 100% superwash merino wool; 1³/₄ oz (50g); 137 yd (125m).

7 (8, 10) balls in #1404 Black

Size H-8 (5mm) crochet hook for sizes S/M and XL

Size I-9 (5.5mm) crochet hook for size L, or hook sizes needed to obtain gauge

Split-ring markers or scraps of contrasting yarn for markers

Purchased sweater clasp

gauge

For sizes S/M and XL, using H-8 (5mm) hook, in patt, one rep = 3" (7.5cm); 6 rows = 3¹/₂" (9cm); 12 BASE CH/SC = 4" (10cm); 13 sc of band = 4" (10cm)

For size L, using I-9 (5.5mm) hook, in patt, one rep = 3¹/₂" (9cm); 6 rows = 3³/₄" (9.5cm); 11 BASE CH/SC = 4" (10cm); 12 sc of band = 4" (10cm)

NOTE: Fabric is very stretchy, so you will need to block each size to measurements.

INSTRUCTIONS

Cardigan is made from the neck down in one piece.

Size S/M uses size H-8 hook throughout; size L uses size I-9 hook throughout. These two sizes have exactly the same instructions.

Size XL uses H-8 hook throughout. Separate instructions for yoke-shaping follow.

yoke

SIZES SMALL/MEDIUM AND LARGE ONLY

BASE CH/SC 37, to measure approximately 12" (30.5cm) slightly stretched.

ROW 1 (RS): Ch 3, 7 dc in first sc, *sk next 2 sc, sc in next sc, ch 5, sk next 2 sc, sc in next sc, sk next 2 sc, SHELL in next sc; rep from * 3 times, turn: 5 shells.

ROW 2 (WS): Ch 8 (counts as dc, ch 5), dc in first dc, (ch 1, dc in next dc) 7 times, *sc in next ch-5 sp, dc in next dc, (ch 1, dc in next dc) 7 times; rep from * 3 times, placing last dc in top of tch, ch 5, dc in same ch, turn. Shape neck and shoulders as follows:

ROW 3 (INC): Ch 8, (dc, ch 5, dc) in first ch-5 sp, *ch 5, sk next ch-1 sp, (sc, ch 5) in each of next 5 ch-1 sps for inc, dc in next sc; rep from * 3 times except omit last dc, instead work (dc, ch 5, dc) in tch sp, ch 5, dc in 3rd ch of tch, turn: 34 ch-5 sps.

ROW 4: Ch 3, 7 dc in first ch-5 sp, *sc in next ch-5 sp, ch 5, sc in next ch-5 sp, SHELL in next ch-5 sp; rep from * 11 times, except omit last SHELL, instead work 7 dc in tch sp, dc in 3rd ch of tch, turn: 12 shells.

ROW 5: Ch 3, dc in first dc, *(ch 1, dc in next dc) 7 times, sc in next ch-5 sp, dc in next dc; rep from * 10 times, (ch 1, dc in next dc) 6 times, ch 1, 2 dc in top of tch, turn.

Make 4 incs evenly spaced as follows:

ROW 6 (INC): Ch 8, sk first 2 ch-1 sps of next shell, sc in next ch-1 sp, ch 5, sk next ch-1 sp, sc in next ch-1 sp, ch 5, sk next 2 ch-1 sps, dc in next sc, ch 5, ** *sk next ch-1 sp, (sc, ch 5) in each of next 5 ch-1 sps for inc, sk next ch-1 sp, dc in next sc, ch 5*, (sk first 2 ch-1 sps of next shell, sc in next ch-1 sp, ch 5, sk next ch-1 sp, sc in next ch-1 sp, ch 5, sk

next 2 ch-1 sps, dc in next sc, ch 5) twice; rep from ** twice; rep from * to * once, sk first 2 ch-1 sps of next shell, sc in next ch-1 sp, ch 5, sk next ch-1 sp, sc in next ch-1 sp, ch 5, sk next 2 ch-1 sps, dc in 3rd ch of tch, turn: 48 ch-5 sps.

ROW 7: Ch 5 (counts as dc, ch 2), sc in first ch-5 sp, *SHELL in next ch-5 sp, sc in next ch-5 sp, ch 5, sc in next ch-5 sp; rep from * 15 times, except omit last ch 5 and sc, instead work ch 2, dc in 3rd ch of tch: 16 shells.

ROW 8: Ch 1, sc in first dc, *dc in next dc, (ch 1, dc in next dc) 7 times, sc in next ch-5 sp; rep from * 15 times, place last sc in 3rd ch of tch, turn.

ROW 9: Ch 8, *sk next 2 ch-1 sp, sc in next ch-1 sp, ch 5, sk next ch-1 sp, sc in next ch-1 sp, ch 5, sk next 2 ch-1 sps, dc in next sc, ch 5; rep from * 15 times, except omit last ch 5, place last dc in last sc, turn.

ROWS 10–11: Rep Rows 7–8.

SIZE EXTRA LARGE ONLY

BASE CH/SC 41, to measure approximately 13½" (34cm) slightly stretched.

XL ROW 1 (RS): Ch 3, 7 dc in first sc, *sk next 2 sc, sc in next sc, ch 5, sk next 3 sc, sc in next sc, sk next 2 sc, SHELL in next sc; rep from * 3 times, turn: 5 shells.

XL ROWS 2–8: Work same as Rows 2–8 of sizes S/M (L).

XL ROW 9 (WS) (INC): Ch 8, (sk first 2 ch-1 sp of next shell, sc in next ch-1 sp, ch 5, sk next

ch-1 sp, sc in next ch-1 sp, ch 5, dc in next sc, ch 5) twice, *sk next 2 ch-1 sp, (sc, ch 5) in each of next 5 ch-1 sps for inc, dc in next sc, ch 5*; (sk first 2 ch-1 sp of next shell, sc in next ch-1 sp, ch 5, sk next ch-1 sp, sc in next ch-1 sp, ch 5, dc in next sc, ch 5) twice; rep from * to * once, (sk first 2 ch-1 sp of next shell, sc in next ch-1 sp, ch 5, sk next ch-1 sp, sc in next ch-1 sp, ch 5, dc in next sc, ch 5) 4 times; rep from * to * once, (sk first 2 ch-1 sp of next shell, sc in next ch-1 sp, ch 5, sk next ch-1 sp, sc in next ch-1 sp, ch 5, dc in next sc, ch 5) twice; rep from * to * once, (sk first 2 ch-1 sp of next shell, sc in next ch-1 sp, ch 5, sk next ch-1 sp, sc in next ch-1 sp, ch 5, dc in next sc, ch 5) twice, except omit last ch 5, place last dc in 3rd ch of tch, turn: 60 ch-5 sps.

XL ROWS 10–11: Work same as Rows 7–8: 20 shells.

XL ROW 12 (INC): Ch 8, (sk first 2 ch-1 sp of next shell, sc in next ch-1 sp, ch 5, sk next ch-1 sp, sc in next ch-1 sp, ch 5, dc in next sc, ch 5) 3 times, *sk next 2 ch-1 sp, (sc, ch 5) in each of next 5 ch-1 sps for inc, dc in next sc, ch 5*; (sk first 2 ch-1 sp of next shell, sc in next ch-1 sp, ch 5, sk next ch-1 sp, sc in next ch-1 sp, ch 5, dc in next sc, ch 5) twice; rep from * to * once, (sk first 2 ch-1 sp of next shell, sc in next ch-1 sp, ch 5, sk next ch-1 sp, sc in next ch-1 sp, ch 5, dc in next sc, ch 5) 6 times; rep from * to * once, (sk first 2 ch-1 sp of next shell, sc in next ch-1 sp, ch 5, sk next ch-1 sp, sc in next ch-1 sp, ch 5, dc in next sc, ch 5) twice; rep from * to * once, (sk first 2 ch-1 sp of next shell, sc in next ch-1 sp, ch 5, sk next ch-1 sp, sc in next ch-1 sp, ch 5, dc in next sc, ch 5) 3 times, except omit last ch 5, work last dc in 3rd ch of tch, turn: 72 ch-5 sps.

XL ROWS 13–14: Work same as Rows 7–8: 24 shells.

body
ALL SIZES

Join fronts and back with additional sts at underarms as follows:

ROW 1 (WS) (JOIN): Ch 8, (sk first 2 ch-1 sp of next shell, sc in next ch-1 sp, ch 5, sk next ch-1 sp, sc in next ch-1 sp, ch 5, dc in next sc, ch 5) 2 (2, 3) times, *sk first 2 ch-1 sp of next shell, sc in next ch-1 sp, ch 5, sk next ch-1 sp, sc in next ch-1 sp, ch 9 for underarm, sk next 2 (2, 4) shells of armhole*, (sk first 2 ch-1 sp of next shell, sc in next ch-1 sp, ch 5, sk next ch-1 sp, sc in next ch-1 sp, ch 5, dc in next sc, ch 5) 5 (5, 7) times; rep from * to *, (sk first 2 ch-1 sp of next shell, sc in next ch-1 sp, ch 5, sk next ch-1 sp, sc in next ch-1 sp, ch 5, dc

in next sc, ch 5) 3 (3, 4) times, except omit last ch 5, work last dc in last sc, turn.

Mark 5th (middle) ch at each underarm for later use.

ROW 2: Ch 5, sc in first ch-5 sp, (SHELL in next ch-5 sp, sc in next ch-5 sp, ch 5, sc in next ch-5 sp) 2 (2, 3) times, *SHELL in next ch-5 sp, sk first ch of underarm, sc in next ch, ch 5, sk next 3 ch of underarm, sc in next ch*; (SHELL in next ch-5 sp, sc in next ch-5 sp, ch 5, sc in next ch-5 sp) 5 (5, 7) times; rep from * to * across other underarm chs, (SHELL in next ch-5 sp, sc in next ch-5 sp, ch 5, sc in next ch-5 sp) 3 (3, 4) times, except omit last ch 5 and sc, instead work ch 2, dc in 3rd ch of tch: 12 (12, 16) shells.

ROW 3: Ch 1, sc in first dc, *dc in next dc, (ch 1, dc in next dc) 7 times, sc in next ch-5 sp*; rep from * 11 (11, 15) times, work last sc in 3rd ch of tch, turn.

ROW 4: Ch 8, *sk next 2 ch-1 sps, sc in next ch-1 sp, ch 5, sk next ch-1 sp, sc in next ch-1 sp, ch 5, dc in next sc, ch 5; rep from * 11 (11, 15) times, except omit last ch 5, working last dc in last sc, turn.

ROW 5: Ch 5, sc in first ch-5 sp, *SHELL in next ch-5 sp, sc in next ch-5 sp, ch 5, sc in next ch-5 sp; rep from * 11 (11, 15) times, except omit last ch 5 and sc, instead work ch 2, dc in 3rd ch of tch: 12 (12, 16) shells.

ROWS 6–12: Rep Rows 3–5 (twice); then rep Row 3 once more.

The next row slightly gathers the lower edge and shapes the waist.

ROW 13 (WS): Ch 6, *sk next 2 ch-1 sp, sc in next ch-1 sp, ch 3, sk next ch-1 sp, sc in next ch-1 sp, ch 3, dc in next sc, ch 3; rep from * 11 (11, 16) times, except omit last ch 5, work last dc in last sc, turn.

finishing

EDGING: With RS facing, continue with edging around entire cardigan.

RND 1 (RS): Ch 1, sc in first dc, (2 sc in next ch-3 sp, sc in next st) across lower edge, 2 sc in tch sp, 3 sc in 3rd ch of tch for corner, rotate and work along front edge, 2 sc in first row-end dc, (sc in next row-end sc, 2 dc in next 2 row-end dc) 6 (6, 7) times, 5 dc in next row-end dc for front neck corner, 2 sc in next 4 row-end dc of neck shaping, sc in 37 (37, 41) base ch of neck, 2 sc in next 4 row-end dc of neck shaping, 5 sc in next row-end dc for neck corner, (2 sc in next 2 row-end dc, sc in next row-end sc) 6 (6, 7) times, 2 sc in last row-end dc, 2 sc in same st as beg for corner, sl st in beg sc, turn.

RND 2 (WS): Ch 1, 3 sc in next sc for corner, sc in each sc around, working 3 sc in middle sc of each corner, sl st in beg sc, turn.

RND 3 (RS): Ch 1, sc in each sc around, working 3 sc in middle sc of each corner, sl st in beg sc, do not turn.

RND 4 (RS): Ch 1, (rev sc in next sc, ch 1, sk next sc) around, except at corners (either before or after middle sc of corner) omit one skipped sc by working (rev sc in next sc, ch 1, rev sc in next sc), sl st in beg sc. Fasten off.

first sleeve

With WS facing, locate marked (middle) underarm ch. Join yarn with sl st in marked ch.

RND 1 (WS): Ch 8, sk next 3 chs of underarm, sc in next ch, ch 5, sc in next ch-1 sp of shell (same ch-1 sp as previously worked for join), now working on skipped shells of armhole, *ch 5, dc in next sc, ch 5, sk first 2 ch-1 sp of next shell, sc in next ch-1 sp, ch 5, sk next ch-1 sp, sc in next ch-1 sp; rep from * 1 (1, 3) times, ch 5, dc in next sc, ch 5, sk first 2 ch-1 sp of next shell, sc in next ch-1 sp (same as previously worked for join), ch 5, sc in next ch of underarm, ch 2, dc in 3rd ch of beg ch, turn.

RND 2: Ch 1, sc in same sp, *SHELL in next ch-5 sp, sc in next ch-5 sp, ch 5, sc in next ch-5 sp; rep from * 3 times, except omit last ch 5 and sc, instead work ch 2, dc in beg sc, turn: 4 (4, 6) shells.

RND 3: Ch 1, sc in same sp, *dc in next dc, (ch 1, dc in next dc) 7 times, sc in next ch-5 sp; rep from * 3 (3, 5) times, except omit last sc, instead sl st in beg sc, turn.

RND 4: Ch 8, *sk first 2 ch-1 sps of next shell, sc in next ch-1 sp, ch 5, sk next ch-1 sp, sc in next ch-1 sp, ch 5, dc in next sc, ch 5; rep from * 3 (3, 5) times, except omit last (ch 5, dc and ch 5), instead work ch 2, dc in 3rd ch of beg ch, turn.

RNDS 5–24: Rep Rnds 2–4 (6 times); then rep Rnds 2–3 once more.

Next rnd slightly gathers bottom of sleeve.

RND 25 (WS): Ch 6, *sk first 2 ch-1 sp of next shell, sc in next ch-1 sp, ch 3, sk next ch-1 sp, sc in next ch-1 sp, ch 3, dc in next sc, ch 3; rep from * 3 (3, 5) times, except omit last (ch 3, dc and ch 3), instead work ch 1, hdc in 3rd ch of beg ch, turn.

RND 26 (RS): Ch 1, sc in same sp, (sc in next st, 2 sc in next ch-3 sp) 11 (11, 17) times, sc in next st, sc in same sp as beg, sl st in beg sc, turn: 36 (36, 54) sc.

RND 27: Ch 1, sc in each sc around, sl st in beg sc, turn.

RND 28: Ch 1, sc in each sc around, sl st in beg sc, do not turn.

RND 29: Ch 1, (rev sc in next sc, ch 1, sk next sc) 18 (18, 27) times, sl st in beg sc. Fasten off.

Rep sleeve and cuff in other armhole in same way.

Weave ends, block cardigan to measurements.

Sew purchased sweater clasp to band at either corner of neck edge.

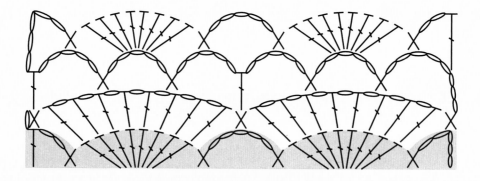

REDUCED SAMPLE OF BASIC SHELL PATTERN

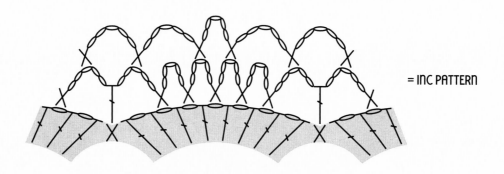

= INC PATTERN

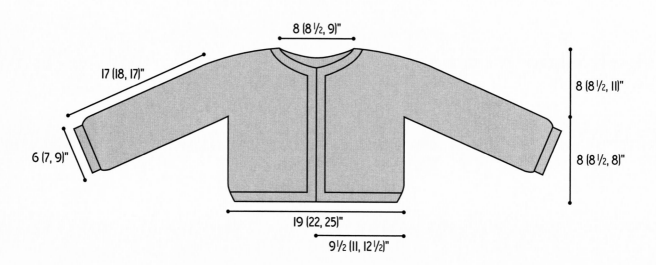

8 (8½, 9)"

17 (18, 17)"

8 (8½, 11)"

6 (7, 9)"

8 (8½, 8)"

19 (22, 25)"

9½ (11, 12½)"

anisette vest

This vest is a glorified scarf, a short take on the Pistachio Parfait ruana (page 109), made in a luxurious silk bouclé yarn. It can be worn level, with the fronts and back even and square, skimming the ribs; it can also be worn rotated to the back, with the fronts pointed to form a V-neck. Feel free to use a brooch, self-yarn string, or whatever you'd like to join and close the fronts as desired.

size

Directions are given for size Small/Medium (S/M). Changes for Large/Extra Large (L/XL) are in parentheses. Sample is size Small/Medium.

Finished bust: 39 (51)" (99 [129.5]cm) with 3" (7.5cm) gap at center front

To fit: 42 (54)" (107 [137]cm) bust

Back length: 12 (15)" (30.5 [38]cm)

materials

Tess' Designer Yarns "Silk Boucle"; 100% silk; 3½ oz (100g); 200 yd (183m)

2 hanks in English Sheepdog (black/gray/white)

Size I-9 (5.5mm) crochet hook

Blunt yarn needle

gauge

In patt, one rep and 6 rows = 3" (7.5cm).

SPECIAL STITCHES

BASE CH/SC: See Introduction.

TRIPLE CURVE STITCH: See Chapter 1, Allegheny Moon Mobius (page 42).

INSTRUCTIONS

Back is 7 (9) reps wide by 4 (5) reps long; divide for fronts with one rep unworked at center back neck, fronts are 3 (4) reps wide by 4 (5) reps long.

back

BASE CH/SC 57 (73), to measure approx 21 (27)" (53.5 [68.5]cm) slightly stretched. Set up 7 (9) patt reps.

Work FOUNDATION ROW, then PATT ROWS 1–6 for 3 (4) times, then PATT ROWS 1–5 once more.

first front

Divide for neck and fronts.

NEXT ROW (SAME AS PATT ROW 6): Ch 1, sc in first 2 sc, *sc in next ch-3 sp, ch 5, sc in next ch-3 sp, sc in next 3 sc; rep from * 2 (3) more times, except omit last sc, turn, leaving rem sts unworked: 3 (4) patt reps for front.

Now working across reps of one front, rep PATT ROWS 1–6 for 3 (4) times, PATT ROWS 1–5 once more.

NEXT ROW (MAKE CH 3 INSTEAD OF CH 5): Ch 1, sc in first 2 sc, *sc in next ch-3 sp, ch 3, sc in next ch-3 sp, sc in next 3 sc; rep from * across, except omit last sc, turn.

LAST ROW: Ch 1, sc in first 3 sc, *3 sc in next ch-3 sp, sc in next 5 sc; rep from * across, except omit last 2 sc. Fasten off.

second front

Return to neck, leave sc at center of neck unworked, join yarn with sl st in next ch-3 sp, ch 1, rep First Front. Weave ends. Lightly block piece before finishing.

finishing

Fold fronts along shoulder line, matching corners at lower sides, matching row edges of front and back at sides. Using yarn and blunt needle, beg from lower corner, whipst tog row edges of sides through both thicknesses, for 3 (4)" (7.5 [10]cm). Fasten off.

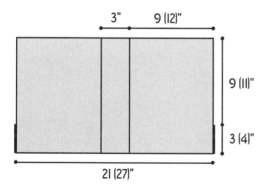

abydos vest

This is a breezy, open-stitch vest, with a scoop neck and deep armholes. Make it cropped or tunic length or any-where in between. I offer here a short version in a rayon/cotton blend that is sensational over a T-shirt and jeans. The long version is in a metallic yarn and looks good over just about anything in basic black.

size

Directions are given for size Small (S). Changes for Medium (M), and Large (L) are in parentheses. Samples are both size Small.

Finished bust: 36 (40, 46)" (91.5 [101.5, 117]cm)

Back length (short version): 15½ (17, 17)" (39.5 [43, 43]cm)

Back length (long version): 29 (31, 31)" (73.5 [79, 79]cm)

materials

For short version: Filatura di Crosa "Brilla"; 42% cotton, 58% rayon; 1¾ oz (50g); 120 yd (110m)

3 (3, 4) balls in #387 (rust)

For long version: Patons "Brilliant"; 69% acrylic, 19% nylon, 12% polyester; 1¾ oz (50g); 166 yd (151m)

4 (5, 6) balls in #3023 Gold Glow

Size G-7 (4.5mm) crochet hook for size Small
Size H-8 (5mm) crochet hook for sizes Medium and Large

gauge

For size Small, in patt, using G-7 (4.5mm) hook, 3 shells = 4" (10 cm); 4 rows = 3½" (9cm); 13 sc = 4" (10cm)

For sizes Medium and Large, in patt, using H-8 (5mm) hook, 3 shells = 4½" 11.5cm); 4 rows = 4" (10cm); 12 sc = 4" (10cm)

NOTE: Hook and gauge are oversized for this yarn, and fabric will be very loose. Keep work relaxed for best results. These yarns do not behave the same when blocked; see schematic for approximate finished dimensions.

SPECIAL STITCHES

BASE CH/SC: See Introduction.

Pattern consists of a RS row of shells, and a WS row of V's.

SHELL: 5 tr in same st or sp.

V-ST: (Tr, ch 3, tr) in same st or sp.

INSTRUCTIONS

Vest is crocheted from the neck down, with fronts worked onto back at shoulders and joined at underarms. Size Small uses size 6–7 (15mm) hook throughout. Sizes Medium and Large use size H-8 (5mm) hook throughout.

NOTE: Sizes Small and Medium have exactly the same instructions, size Large begins with more sts in the back neck and has additional sts at the underarms.

back

BASE CH/SC 37 (37, 41) to measure 11 (12, 12½)" (28 [30.5, 32]cm) slightly stretched.

ROW 1 (RS): Ch 4 (counts as tr), 2 tr in first sc, *sk next 3 sc, SHELL in next sc; rep from * 8 (8, 9) times, 3 tr in last sc, turn: 8 (8, 9) shells; 2 half shells.

ROW 2 (WS): Ch 5 (counts as tr, ch 1), tr in first tr, V-st in 3rd (middle) tr of next 8 (8, 9) shells, (tr, ch 1, tr) in top of tch, turn.

ROW 3: Ch 4, 2 tr in first ch-1 sp, SHELL in next 8 (8, 9) ch-3 sps, 2 tr in tch sp, tr in 4th ch of tch, turn.

ROWS 4–5: Rep Rows 2–3. Shape armhole edges as follows:

ROW 6: Ch 7 (counts as tr, ch 3), tr in first tr, V-st in 3rd tr of next 8 (8, 9) shells, V-st in top of tch, turn.

ROW 7: Ch 4, SHELL in next 9 (9, 10) ch-3 sps, SHELL in tch sp, tr in 4th ch of tch, turn; 10 (10, 11) shells.

ROW 8: Ch 7, tr in first tr, V-st in 3rd tr of next 10 (10, 11) shells, V-st in top of tch. Fasten off.

right front

Work Right Front onto last 9 chs of base ch on neck edge.

ROW 1 (WS): With WS of Back facing, sk first 28 (28, 32) ch on neck edge of Back, join yarn with sl st in next ch, ch 5, tr in same ch, sk next 3 ch sts, V-st in next ch, sk next 3 ch sts, (tr, ch 1, tr) in last ch, turn.

ROW 2 (RS): Ch 4, 2 tr in first ch-1 sp, SHELL in next ch-3 sp, 2 tr in tch sp, tr in 4th ch of tch, turn.

ROW 3: Ch 5, tr in first tr, V-st in 3rd tr of next shell, (tr, ch 1, tr) in top of tch, turn.

ROWS 4–6: Rep Rows 2–3; then rep Row 2 once more. Fasten off.

left front

Work Left Front onto first 9 chs of base ch.

ROW 1 (WS): With WS of back facing, join yarn with sl st in first ch on neck edge of Back, ch 5, tr in same ch, sk next 3 ch, V-st in next ch, (tr, ch 1, tr) in next ch, turn.

ROWS 2–6: Rep Rows 2–6 of Right Front. Do not fasten off, turn to work next row to join fronts.

ROW 7: Ch 5, tr in first tr, V-st in 3rd tr of next shell, V-st in top of tch, ch 1, BASE CH/SC 19 (19, 23) for front neck, V-st in first tr of Left Front, V-st in 3rd tr of next shell, (tr, ch 1, tr) in top of tch, turn.

ROW 8: Ch 4, 2 tr in first ch-1 sp, SHELL in next 2 ch-3 sp, *sk next 3 sc of front neck, SHELL in next sc; rep from * 3 (3, 4) times, SHELL in next 2 ch-3 sps, 2 tr in tch sp, tr in 4th ch of tch, turn: 8 (8, 9) shells; 2 half shells. Shape armhole edges as follows:

ROW 9: Ch 7, tr in first tr, V-st in 3rd tr of next 8 (8, 9) shells, V-st in top of tch, turn.

ROW 10: Ch 4, SHELL in next 9 (9, 10) ch-3 sp, SHELL in tch sp, tr in 4th ch of tch, turn: 10 (10, 11) shells.

ROW 11: Ch 7 (counts as tr, ch 3), tr in first tr, V-st in 3rd tr of next 10 (10, 11) shells, V-st in top of tch, turn.

Join Front and Back with additional sts at underarms.

JOINING ROW (RS): Ch 4, 4 tr in first ch-3 sp, *SHELL in next 10 (10, 11) ch-3 sps, 4 tr in tch sp, tr in 4th ch of tch, ch 1, BASE CH/SC 7 (7, 11) for underarm*, tr in first tr of Back, 4 tr in first ch-3 sp; rep from * to * once, sl st in top of beg ch, sl st in next 2 tr, turn.

body

Work in joined rnds for remainder of body.

RND 1 (WS): Ch 4, *(sk next 3 sc of underarm, V-st in next sc) 1 (1, 2) times, V-st in 3rd tr of next 12 (12, 13) shells; rep from *, except omit last V-st, instead work tr in same tr as beg, ch 1, hdc in top of beg ch, turn.

RND 2 (RS): Ch 4, 2 tr in same sp, SHELL in next 25 (25, 29) ch-3 sps, 2 tr in same sp as beg, sl st in top of beg ch, turn: 26 (26, 30) shells.

RND 3: Ch 4, V-st in 3rd tr of next 25 (25, 29) shells, tr in same st as beg, ch 1, hdc in top of beg ch, turn.

SHORT VERSION

RND 4–6: Rep Rnds 2–3; then rep Rnd 2 once more. Fasten off.

LONG VERSION

RNDS 4–20: Rep Rnds 2–3 (8 times), rep Rnd 2 once more.

Fasten off.
(Alternately, work to desired length, ending with Rnd 2 of patt.)
Weave ends.

finishing

Work one rnd of sc at armholes and neck.

NECK EDGING: With RS of neck edge facing, join yarn with sl st in first unworked base ch at back neck, ch 1, sc in same ch, sc in rem 18 (18, 22) ch sts, 3 sc in next 7 row-end tr of front, sc in 19 (19, 23) chs of front neck, 3 sc in next 7 row-end tr of front, sl st in top of beg sc. Fasten off.

ARMHOLE EDGING: With RS of one armhole facing, join yarn with sl st in center ch of underarm, ch 1, sc in same ch, sc in next 3 (3, 5) chs, 3 sc in next 21 row-end tr of armhole, sc in next 3 (3, 5) chs of underarm, sl st in beg sc. Fasten off.

Rep armhole edging around other armhole.

Weave ends, and lightly block to measurements.

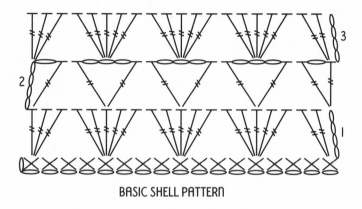

BASIC SHELL PATTERN

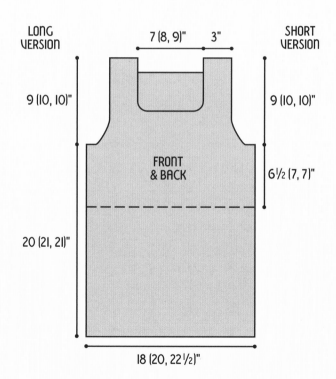

LONG VERSION

7 (8, 9)"   3"

SHORT VERSION

9 (10, 10)"

9 (10, 10)"

FRONT & BACK

6½ (7, 7)"

20 (21, 21)"

18 (20, 22½)"

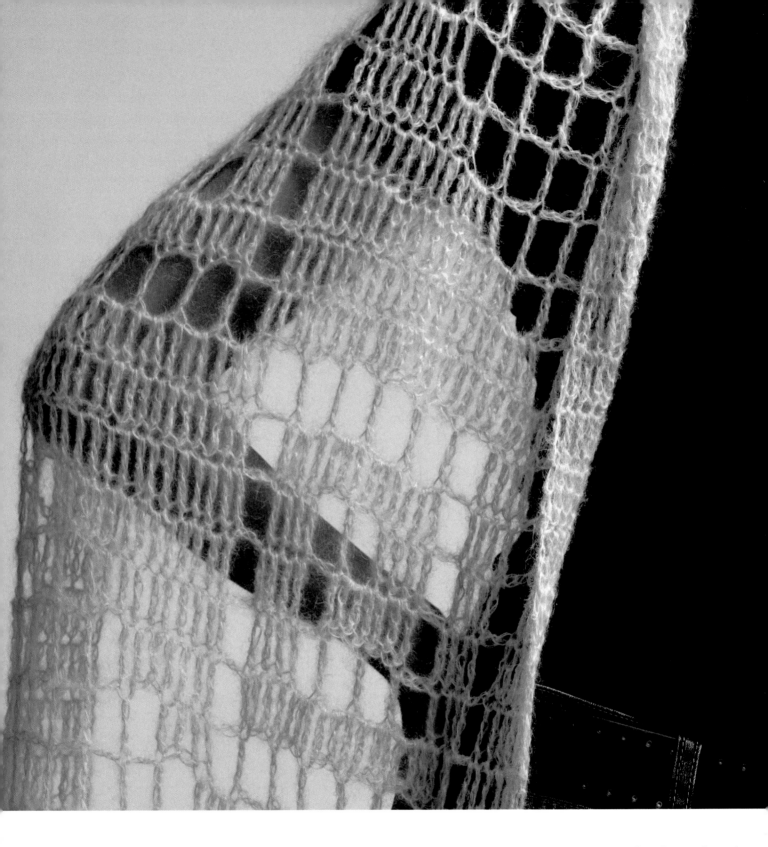

irish mist stole

Lace-weight mohair is often knitted and crocheted into ethereal shawls . . . by people with a lot of patience. I wanted a wrap that was light as a cloud but also easy and quick to crochet. The solution—doubling the yarn and super-sizing the hook—produced this lovely shawl made in exploded filet crochet, inspired by a Celtic-style border motif.

SUPER FINE 1

size

One size fits all

20 x 80" (51x203cm).

materials

Filatura di Crosa "Baby Kid Extra"; 80% Kid Mohair, 20% Nylon; 0.87 oz (25g); 268 yd (245m)

5 balls in #426 (butter)

Size J-10 (6mm) crochet hook

Yarn needle

gauge

With 2 strands of yarn held tog as one, 4 blocks and 4 rows in tr filet = approx 4" (10cm)

NOTE: Stole will grow a couple of inches in length when complete.

SPECIAL STITCHES

BASE CH/SC: See Introduction

FILET CROCHET:

One block = 3 tr

One mesh = ch 2, tr

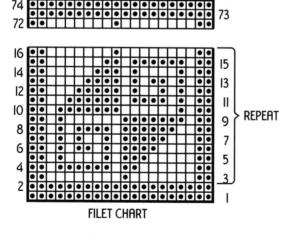

FILET CHART

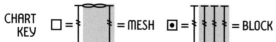

CHART KEY   □ = MESH   ▣ = BLOCK

INSTRUCTIONS

NOTE: Yarn is held doubled throughout.

Stole is rectangular, 20 blocks wide by 74 blocks long, plus sc edge. The FILET pattern is 14 blocks long, repeated 5 times.

Holding 2 strands of yarn tog, BASE CH/SC 61 for 20 blocks plus edge st.

ROW 1 (RS): Ch 4 (counts as tr), sk first sc, tr in next 60 sc, turn: (Row 1 of FILET chart complete) 61 tr; 20 blocks.

ROW 2: Ch 4, sk first tr, tr in next 59 tr, tr in top of tch, turn: (Row 2 of FILET chart complete) 61 tr, 20 blocks.

ROWS 3–16: Work in blocks and meshes following Rows 3–16 of FILET chart.

ROWS 17–72: Rep Rows 3–16 (5 times).

ROW 73 (SOLID BLOCKS): Ch 4, sk first tr, tr in next 6 tr, *2 tr in next ch-sp, tr in next tr*; rep from * to * 6 times, tr in next 3 tr, rep from * to * 8 times, tr in next 5 tr, tr in top of tch, turn: (Row 73 of FILET chart complete) 61 tr; 20 blocks.

ROW 74: Rep Row 2: 61 tr; 20 blocks.

edging

ROW 75: Ch 1, sc in first tr, sc in next 59 tr, sc in top of tch. Fasten off.

Weave ends.

blue curaçao shawl

There is renewed interest in heirloom crochet stitches such as the pineapple. The pineapple shape, wide at the base and dwindling to nothing at the tip, is tricky but not impossible to manipulate. I exploded an old-fashioned pineapple dresser scarf into this shawl, shaped somewhere in between a triangle and a three-quarters circle, with extra room through the shoulder to help it stay on. This new yarn offers a mohair look and lofty feel without the shedding, a wool blend shot with a lustrous rayon component that gives the fabric extra depth and interest.

size

One size fits most

Center back length: approx 25" (63.5cm)

Length across front edge: approx 60" (152.5cm)

materials

Lily Chin Signature Collection "Greenwich Village"; 26% wool, 21% acrylic, 48% polyester, 5% viscose; 1³/4 oz (50g); 138 yd (126m)

5 balls in #5579 (blue)

Size I-9 (5.5mm) crochet hook

Yarn needle

gauge

Gauge is difficult to measure.

After completing Rows 1–2 (both sides of foundation ch worked), piece = approximately 1¹/2 x 6" (4x15cm). 4 rows of shells in patt = approximately 3³/4" (9.5cm)

NOTE: Gauge is not critical. Fabric will not grow excessively with blocking, so keep the work relaxed for the airiest effect and to obtain a reasonably sized shawl.

SPECIAL STITCHES

SHELL: (2 dc, ch 1, 2 dc) in same st or sp.

INC SHELL (increase): (2 dc, ch 1, 2 dc, ch 1, 2 dc) in same sp.

SCALLOP: Ch 4, 2 tr in 4th ch from hook.

INSTRUCTIONS

Shawl is crocheted from the top down, shaped by increases in pattern across the shoulder, at center back, and at front edges.

The shawl creates its own edging as you go, so there is no finishing!

Ch 21 for foundation.

ROW 1 (NECK EDGING): Tr in 5th ch from hook, *sk next 3 ch, (sl st, ch 4, tr) in next ch; rep from * twice, sl st in last ch, do not turn. Rotate and continue along opposite side of foundation ch.

ROW 2: Ch 3, dc in same ch, ch 1, 2 dc in next ch, (ch 1, sk next ch, 2 dc in next ch) 7 times, ch 1, 2 dc in spare lp of last ch, turn: 9 ch-1 sps.

Set up 4 pineapple reps as follows:

ROW 3: Ch 2, *SHELL in next ch-1 sp, ch 4, sc in next ch-1 sp, ch 4; rep from * 3 times, SHELL in last ch-1 sp, turn: 5 shells, 4 reps.

ROW 4: Ch 2, *SHELL in ch-sp of next shell, ch 4, sc in next ch-4 sp, ch 5, sc in next ch-4 sp, ch

4; rep from * 3 times, SHELL in ch-sp of last shell, turn.

ROW 5: Ch 2, *SHELL in ch-sp of next shell, ch 3, sc in next ch-4 sp, 7 dc in next ch-5 sp, sc in next ch-4 sp, ch 3; rep from * 3 times, SHELL in ch-sp of last shell, turn.

ROW 6: Ch 2, *SHELL in ch-sp of next shell, ch 3, sc in next ch-3 sp, dc in next dc, (ch 1, dc in next dc) 6 times, sc in next ch-3 sp, ch 3; rep from * 3 times, SHELL in ch-sp of last shell, turn.

Begin to close original 4 pineapples, set up increase to 8 pineapple reps as follows:

ROW 7: Ch 2, INC SHELL in ch-sp of next shell, *ch 3, sk next ch-3 sp, (sc in next ch-1 sp, ch 3) 6 times, sk next ch-3 sp**, (SHELL, ch 1, SHELL) in ch-sp of next shell; rep from * twice; rep from * to ** once, INC SHELL in ch-sp of last shell, turn.

ROW 8: Ch 2, SHELL in next 2 ch-1 sp, *ch 3, sk next ch-3 sp, (sc in next ch-3 sp, ch 3) 5 times, sk next ch-3 sp, SHELL in next 3 ch-1 sp; rep from * 3 times, except omit last shell, turn.

ROW 9: Ch 2, *SHELL in ch-sp of next shell, ch 1, SHELL in ch-sp of next shell, ch 3, sk next ch-3 sp, (sc in next ch-3 sp, ch 3) 4 times, sk next ch-3 sp, SHELL in ch-sp of next shell, ch 1; rep from * 3 times, SHELL in ch-sp of last shell, turn.

ROW 10: Ch 2, *SHELL in ch-sp of next shell, ch 4, sc in next ch-1 sp bet shells, ch 4, SHELL in ch-sp of next shell, ch 3, sk next ch-3 sp, (sc in next ch-3 sp, ch 3) 3 times, ch 3, sk next ch-3 sp, SHELL in ch-sp of next shell, ch 4, sc in next ch-1 sp bet shells, ch 4; rep from * 3 times, SHELL in ch-sp of last shell, turn.

ROW 11: Ch 2, *SHELL in ch-sp of next shell, ch 4, sc in next ch-4 sp, ch 5, sc in next ch-4 sp, ch 4*, **SHELL in ch-sp of next shell, ch 3, sk next ch-3 sp, (sc in next ch-3 sp, ch 3) twice, sk next ch-3 sp***; rep from * to * twice; rep from ** twice; rep from ** to *** once, SHELL in ch-sp of last shell, turn.

ROW 12: Ch 2, *SHELL in ch-sp of next shell, ch 3, sc in next ch-4 sp, 7 dc in next ch-5 sp, sc in next ch-4 sp, ch 3*; **SHELL in ch-sp of next shell, ch 3, sk next ch-3 sp, sc in next ch-3 sp, ch 3, sk next ch-3 sp; rep from * to * twice; rep from ** 3 times, omitting last rep from * to *, SHELL in ch-sp of last shell, turn: 8 pineapple bases.

ROW 13: Ch 2, SHELL in ch-sp of next shell, *ch 3, sc in next ch-3 sp, dc in next dc, (ch 1, dc in next dc) 6 times, sc in next ch-3 sp, ch 3, SHELL in ch-sp of next shell*, **sk next 2 ch-3 sps to close pineapple, SHELL in ch-sp of next shell; rep from * to * twice; rep from

** 3 times, omitting last rep from * to *, turn.

Begin to close 8 pineapples, set up increases to 10 pineapple reps as follows:

ROW 14: Ch 2, INC SHELL in ch-sp of next shell, ** *ch 3, sk next ch-3 sp, (sc in next ch-1 sp, ch 3) 6 times, sk next ch-3 sp*, SHELL in ch-sp of next 2 shells; rep from * to * once **, INC SHELL in ch-sp of next shell; rep from ** to ** once, (SHELL, ch 1, SHELL) in ch-sp of next shell for center back; rep from ** to ** once, INC SHELL in ch-sp of next shell; rep from ** to ** once; INC SHELL in ch-sp of last shell, turn.

ROW 15: Ch 2, *SHELL in next 2 ch-1 sps, ch 3, sk next ch-3 sp, (sc in next ch-3 sp, ch 3) 5 times, sk next ch-3 sp*; rep from * to * 3 times, SHELL in next ch-1 (inc at center back); rep from * to * 4 times, SHELL in next 2 ch-1 sp, turn.

ROW 16: Ch 2, *SHELL in ch-sp of next shell, ch 1, SHELL in ch-sp of next shell, ch 3, sk next ch-3 sp, (sc in next ch-3 sp, ch 3) 4 times*; rep from * to * 3 times, SHELL in ch-sp of next shell, ch 1 (inc at center back); rep from * to * 4 times, SHELL in ch-sp of next shell, ch 1, SHELL in ch-sp of last shell, turn.

ROW 17: Ch 2, ** *SHELL in ch-sp of next shell, ch 4, sc in next ch-1 sp bet shells, ch 4*,

SHELL in ch-sp of next shell, ch 3, sk next ch-3 sp, (sc in next ch-3 sp, ch 3) 3 times, sk next ch-3 sp**; rep from ** to ** 3 times; rep from * to * once; rep from ** to ** 4 times; rep from * to * once, SHELL in ch-sp of last shell, turn.

ROW 18: Ch 2, ** *SHELL in ch-sp of next shell, ch 4, sc in next ch-4 sp, ch 5, sc in next ch-4 sp, ch 4*, SHELL in ch-sp of next shell, ch 3, sk next ch-3 sp, (sc in next ch-3 sp, ch 3) 2 times, sk next ch-3 sp**; rep from ** to ** 3 times; rep from * to * once; rep from ** to ** 4 times; rep from * to * once, SHELL in ch-sp of last shell, turn.

ROW 19: Ch 2, ** *SHELL in ch-sp of next shell, ch 3, sc in next ch-4 sp, 7 dc in next ch-5 sp, sc in next ch-4 sp, ch 3*, SHELL in ch-sp of next shell, ch 3, sk next ch-3 sp, sc in next ch-3 sp, ch 3, sk next ch-3 sp**; rep from ** to ** 3 times rep from * to * once; rep from ** to ** 4 times; rep from * to * once, SHELL in ch-sp of last shell, turn: 10 pineapple bases.

ROW 20: Ch 2, *SHELL in ch-sp of next shell, ch 3, sc in next ch-3 sp, dc in next dc, (ch 1, dc in next dc) 6 times, sc in next ch-3 sp, ch 3**, SHELL in ch-sp of next shell, next 2 ch-3 sps*; rep from * to * 3 times; rep from * to ** once; rep from * to * 5 times, ending with SHELL in ch-sp of last shell, turn.

Begin to close 10 pineapples, set up increases at fronts and center back as follows:

ROW 21: Ch 2, (SHELL, ch 1, SHELL) in ch-sp of next shell, ** *ch 3, sk next ch-3 sp, (sc in next ch-1 sp, ch 3) 6 times, skip next ch-3 sp*, SHELL in ch-sp of next shell, ch 1, SHELL in ch-sp of next shell**; rep from ** to ** 3 times; rep from * to * once, (SHELL, ch 1, SHELL) in ch-1 sp at center back; rep from ** to ** 4 times; rep from * to * once, (SHELL, ch 1, shell) in ch-sp of last shell, turn.

ROW 22: Ch 2, ** *SHELL in ch-sp of next shell, ch 4, sc in next ch-1 sp bet shells, ch 4, SHELL in ch-sp of next shell*, ch 3, sk next ch-3 sp, (sc in next ch-3 sp, ch 3) 5 times, sk next ch-3 sp; rep from ** to ** 9 times; rep from * to * once, turn.

ROW 23: Ch 2, ** *SHELL in ch-sp of next shell, ch 4, sc in next ch-4 sp, ch 5, sc in next ch-4 sp, ch 4, SHELL in ch-sp of next shell*, ch 3, sk next ch-3 sp, (sc in next ch-3 sp, ch 3) 4 times, sk next ch-3 sp; rep from ** to ** 9 times; rep from * to * once, turn.

ROW 24: Ch 2, ** *SHELL in ch-sp of next shell, ch 3, sc in next ch-4 sp, 7 dc in next ch-5 sp, sc in next ch-4 sp, ch 3, SHELL in ch-sp of next shell*, ch 3, sk next ch-3 sp, (sc in next ch-3 sp, ch 3) 3 times, sk next ch-3 sp; rep from ** to

** 9 times; rep from * to * once, turn: 11 web bases.

ROW 25: Ch 2, ** *SHELL in ch-sp of next shell, ch 3, sc in next ch-3 sp, dc in next dc, (ch 1, dc in next dc) 6 times, sc in next ch-3 sp, ch 3, SHELL in ch-sp of next shell*, ch 3, sk next ch-3 sp, (sc in next ch-3 sp, ch 3) twice, sk next ch-3 sp; rep from ** to ** 9 times; rep from * to * once, turn.

ROW 26: Ch 2, ** *SHELL in ch-sp of next shell, ch 3, sc in next ch-3 sp, dc in next dc, (ch 2, dc in next dc) 6 times, sc in next ch-3 sp, ch 3, SHELL in ch-sp of next shell*, ch 3, sk next ch-3 sp, sc in next ch-3 sp, ch 3, sk next ch-3 sp; rep from ** to ** 9 times; rep from * to * once, turn.

ROW 27: Ch 2, *SHELL in ch-sp of next shell, ch 3, sc in next ch-3 sp, dc in next dc, (ch 3, dc in next dc) 6 times, sc in next ch-3 sp, ch 3, SHELL in ch-sp of next shell, sk next 2 ch-3 sps; rep from * to * 11 times, turn.

ROW 28: Ch 2, SHELL in ch-sp of next shell, ch 3, *sc in next ch-3 sp, dc in next dc, (ch 4, dc in next dc) 6 times, sc in next ch-3 sp**, ch 4, sc in sp bet next 2 shells, ch 4; rep from * to * 10 times; rep from * to ** once, ch 3, SHELL in ch-sp of last shell, turn.

ROW 29: Ch 1, sc in first dc, SCALLOP, sc in next ch-3 sp, *(SCALLOP, dc in next dc) 7 times, SCALLOP, sk next sc, sc

in next sc bet shells*; rep from
* to * 9 times, (SCALLOP, dc
in next dc) 7 times, SCALLOP,
sc in next ch-3 sp, SCALLOP,
sc in last dc of shell. Fasten
off.

Weave ends and block to
measurements.

Dampen shawl and lay flat on
a large towel. Do not overly
stretch. Smooth into shape,
roughly a three-quarters circle.

ROWS 1–15

ROWS 15–29

ROWS 15–21
CENTER BACK POINT

THE YARNS

A variety of yarns appear in this book, from the plain to the extraordinary. Please feel free to swap the suggested yarns for your own favorites. Each pattern has a ball band symbol that will help you choose wisely. And don't be afraid to dream up your own component yarn by holding together two or more strands of the same (or different) thin yarns. Ultimately, any yarn, fiber, color, and combination can be used as long as you achieve the gauge for the project.

If the yarns featured in this book are not available at your local shop, visit the websites below to order yarn directly and to find store locators.

BERROCO
508-278-2527
www.berroco.com

CLASSIC ELITE YARNS
978-453-2837
www.classiceliteyarns.com

COATS & CLARK
Distributor of TLC Yarns
800-648-1479
www.coatsandclark.com

LILY CHIN SIGNATURE COLLECTION
Distributed by A2Z Fibers
877-244-1204
www.lilychinsignaturecollection.com

LION BRAND YARNS
800-258-9276
www.lionbrand.com

N.Y. YARNS
888-505-3475
www.nyyarns.com

PATONS
888-368-8401
www.patonsyarns.com

SOUTH WEST TRADING COMPANY
866-794-1818
www.soysilk.com

TAHKI STACY CHARLES, INC.
Distributor of Tahki, S. Charles and Filatura Di Crosa yarns
800-338-YARN
www.tahkistacycharles.com

TESS' DESIGNER YARNS
207-546-2483
www.tessyarns.com

The sweater clasp for Sambuca Jacket, 2 1/2" "Classic Clasp," is available from:

BLACK WATER ABBEY YARNS
720-320-1003
www.abbeyyarns.com

BOOKS

Here's a list of books I found myself delving into during the designing and writing of this book.

For crochet stitch inspiration:

Barnden, Betty. *The Crochet Stitch Bible.* London: Chrysalis Books Group, 2004.

Brittain, Susan, and Karen Manthey. *Crocheting for Dummies.* Indianapolis: Wiley Publishing, Inc., 2004.

Chin, Lily M. *Knit and Crochet with Beads.* Loveland, CO: Interweave Press, 2004.

Elmore, William. *More Elmore.* Big Sandy, TX: Annie's Attic Press, Inc., 1994.

Kooler, Donna. *Donna Kooler's Encyclopedia of Crochet.* Little Rock, AK: Leisure Arts, 2002.

McCall's Needlework Treasury. New York: Random House, 1950.

300 Crochet Stitches, vol. 6. (The Harmony Guides). London: Collins & Brown Ltd., 1998.

220 More Crochet Stitches, vol. 7. (The Harmony Guides). London: Collins & Brown Ltd., 1998.

For thread and lace inspiration:

Any material on thread crochet from living legend Rita Weiss

Any issue of the periodical *Magic Crochet,* Les Editions de Saxe S.A.

Waldrep, Mary Carolyn. *150 Favorite Crochet Designs.* Minneola, NY: Dover Publications, Inc., 1995.

Orr, Ann. *Crochet Designs of Ann Orr.* Minneola, NY: Dover Publications, Inc., 1978.

LINKS

Since discovering my true calling, I have done something I never thought I would do . . . join. With the exception of my mom, my enjoyment of crochet has always been a solitary experience. Today, as a proud member of the Crochet Guild of America (CGOA), I attend and continue to enjoy crochet and fiber-arts events and classes. Through CGOA, I've befriended and worked with the coolest and most eccentric bunch of designers, teachers, editors, and fellow yarn-a-holics.

For info about membership, courses, Chain Link events, and all things crochet:

CROCHET GUILD OF AMERICA
1100-H Brandywine Blvd.
Zanesville, OH 43701-7303
(740) 452-4541 www.crochet.org

Sources for Yarn Standards and Guidelines, event information, and how-to's:

CRAFT & HOBBY ASSOCIATION (CHA)
www.hobby.org

CRAFT YARN COUNCIL OF AMERICA
www.craftyarncouncil.com

THE NATIONAL NEEEDLEARTS ASSOCIATION (TTNA)
www.tnna.org

Since 2003, my designs have appeared in the following publications or in yarn ads in the following:

CROCHET! MAGAZINE
800-449-0440
www.crochetmagazine.com

CROCHET TODAY
800-628-8047
www.crochettoday.com

INTERWEAVE CROCHET
800-272-2193
www.interweavecrochet.com

KNIT.1 (*Vogue Knitting*'s trendy little sister)
877-860-6164
www.knit1mag.com

KNITSCENE
800-272-2193
www.knitscene.com

KNITTER'S MAGAZINE (XRX BOOKS)
800-232-5648
www.knittinguniverse.com

VOGUE KNITTING
646-336-3960(f)
www.vogueknitting.com

INDEX